barbecue

delicious sizzlers

Lorraine Turner & Linda Doeser

This is a Parragon Publishing Book
This edition published in 2005

Parragon Publishing
Queen Street House
4 Queen Street
Bath BA1 1HE
United Kingdom

Produced by
The Bridgewater Book Company
Lewes, East Sussex
United Kingdom BN7 2NZ

Photographer Calvey Taylor-Haw
Home Economists Michaela Haw & Ruth Pollock

ISBN 1-40543-265-9
Printed in China

Notes for the reader

o This book uses imperial, metric, or US cup measurements. Follow the same
   units of measurement throughout; do not mix imperial and metric.
o All spoon measurements are level: teaspoons are assumed to be 5 ml, and
   tablespoons are assumed to be 15 ml.
o Unless otherwise stated, milk is assumed to be whole, eggs and individual
   vegetables such as carrots are medium, and pepper is freshly ground
   black pepper.
o Recipes using raw eggs should be avoided by infants, the elderly, pregnant
   women, convalescents, and anyone suffering from an illness.

Contents

Introduction

There is something wonderfully evocative about the aroma of barbecued food: it can conjure up memories of lazy summer evenings on the beach, delicious aromas wafting from a campfire in the countryside and, most of all, leisurely meals with family and friends in the garden.

Barbecuing is a relaxed way of entertaining, and makes it easy to feed large numbers of guests. You can opt for an informal barbecue party or, if you prefer, a more elaborate affair. Informal ones need no more than a few sausages, burgers, and chicken kabobs, served with a selection of salads, and can be put together at a few moments' notice. When entertaining more formally, you can really go to town on imaginative meat and seafood brochettes, and experiment with marinades.

Although a barbecue may seem a very meat-oriented feast, vegetarians needn't feel left out—vegetables make tasty and colorful kabobs and can be supplemented by jacket potatoes with sour cream and chopped chives, different salsas, and dips. Make sure you also have plenty of substantial salads on offer, such as pasta or mixed bean-based salads if you are expecting vegetarian guests. Children will also appreciate a plentiful supply of French fries.

Serve a choice of soft drinks as well as beer or wine: mineral water, fruit juices, or iced tea will all be welcome. Barbecued food is all about flavor and succulence. With practise, you will learn how best to cook meat, fish, and vegetables on your barbecue, so the result is tender and tasty. Practise makes perfect so use your barbecue frequently!

Equipment

There is a wide range of barbecues available, and several different kinds of fuel. Decide which type suits your particular requirements best. You do not have to spend a vast amount of money. Cheaper barbecues can be just as effective as more expensive ones. Remember: the quality of the food, and the way in which it is marinated and cooked, are more important than the equipment.

Types of barbecue

Popular barbecue options include:

◆ Portable barbecues—these are very convenient in that they can be folded and stored in the trunk of a car.

◆ Disposable barbecues—widely available, these are cheap foil trays with just enough fuel for one hour, enough for one small barbecue.

◆ Brazier barbecues—these can be moved around the garden, and can be stored in the shed. Choose one with a hood, especially if your garden is likely to be windy. Make sure yours is high enough to suit you, or whoever is going to cook on it. If it is too low, you will find it uncomfortable to use for long periods.

◆ Gas and electric barbecues—expensive but quick to warm up and very easy to use. Food cooked on them does not, however, have the traditional "barbecued" flavor, because no charcoal is used.

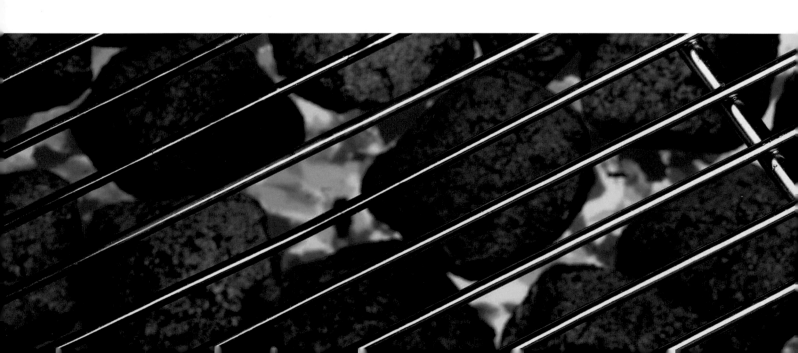

◆ Kettle-grill barbecues—the perfect choice if the weather is unpredictable, because the lid covers the grill.

◆ Permanent, custom-built barbecues—these are excellent if you are very keen on barbecuing and do so frequently. You can have one built for you, using bricks and a metal rack, or build one yourself from a kit.

Types of fuel

Here are some of the choices of fuel to use on your barbecue:

◆ Lumpwood charcoal—although this burns quickly, it is inexpensive, widely available, and easy to light.

◆ Charcoal briquettes—widely available in supermarkets, these are convenient to use in that they burn for quite a long time and produce little smoke.

◆ Easy-to-light charcoal—this is lumpwood charcoal or charcoal briquettes that have been coated in a flammable chemical to make them easy to light. You have to wait until the chemical has burned off before you start to cook, or it will contaminate the food.

◆ Wood fires—give off a wonderful fragrance but need to be carefully supervised. For the best results, choose slow-burning hardwoods, such as apple or oak. Softwoods burn too quickly.

◆ Wood chips and herbs—can be sprinkled over the fire to produce additional fragrance.

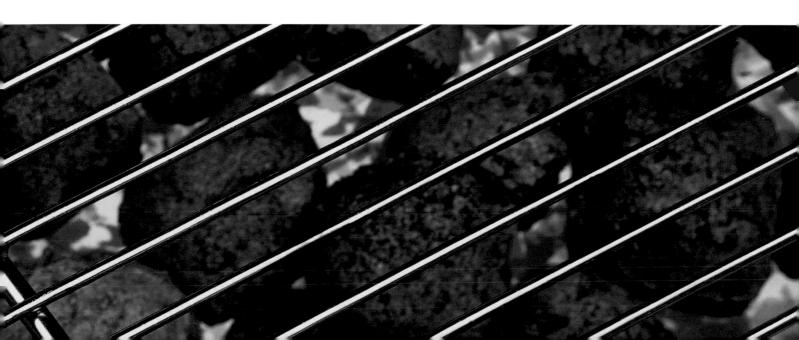

Preparation tips

Although barbecuing is an easy and relaxed way of cooking, you will find it helpful to be as organized as possible. Arrange all the food to be barbecued on trays or large platters and have clean trays and platters ready to take the cooked food when it is barbecued. Enlist a helper or two to assist you in this. Remember to provide tomato ketchup, mustard, barbecue relishes, and any other sauces your guests would enjoy, together with lots of burger buns and a selection of breads. Keep desserts simple: barbecue fruit in foil packages or serve fresh fruit and a generous, varied cheeseboard. If you are barbecuing frozen food, make sure it is thoroughly thawed before you start cooking.

◆ Food to be marinated should ideally be prepared the day before, so it can absorb the marinade flavors fully.

◆ Light your barbecue at least one hour before you start cooking so it can be really hot. Follow the fuel manufacturer's instructions exactly for safety and best results.

◆ Ensure you have all the appropriate equipment, such as oven mitts, long tongs, and spatulas, for turning food over during cooking.

◆ Do not overcrowd the metal rack, or food will not cook evenly and thoroughly through to the center.

◆ Keep similar foods together while cooking, and do not mix meat, fish, and vegetables.

◆ Assemble and dress salads at the last minute for maximum freshness and to prevent the leaves going soggy.

Safety tips

Barbecuing is perfectly safe providing you are sensible and follow a few basic guidelines to ensure personal safety and hygiene. Be scrupulous about knives, cutting boards, and other equipment that may have come into contact with raw meat or fish, and do not allow them to cross-contaminate cooked ingredients. Make sure all your utensils, and the barbecue rack, are clean before you start to cook. Always abide by the safety instructions that come with your barbecue, and be careful around naked flames and fuel.

◆ Keep children and pets well away from the barbecue area, and never leave the barbecue unattended at any time.

◆ Position your barbecue so that it is nowhere near any overhanging trees and shrubs and choose a spot where the smoke will not be a nuisance to other people.

◆ Trim excess fat off any meat to be cooked on the barbecue and shake off excess marinade. If fat is allowed to drip onto the coals, it can ignite.

◆ Keep raw meat away from salads and cooked foods.

◆ Cover all food with cloths to keep insects away.

◆ Do not drink to excess if you are in charge of the barbecue. Carelessness around a barbecue can cause accidents.

Summer wouldn't be summer without barbecues, and this book contains a wide variety of delicious recipes to inspire you. Sausages and simple burgers certainly have their place in a barbecue, and children wouldn't be without them, but do experiment with more inventive recipes incorporating fish, poultry and meat, and vegetables. Food is easy to cook on a barbecue, so be bold and venture forth!

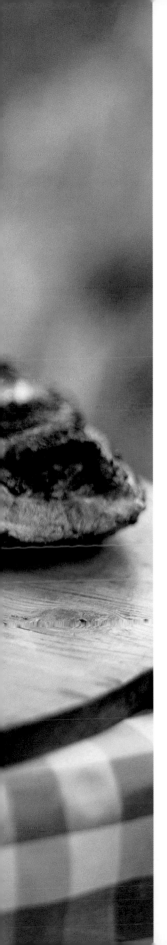

poultry AND meat

Various different meats and poultry can be cooked on the barbecue, for they lend themselves very successfully to this easy method of cooking. The poultry and meat recipes in this section are all simple to prepare and quick to cook, and the variety of accompanying ingredients and tasty marinades will enable you to create an exciting selection of delectable dishes for you to share with your guests.

This is the perfect choice for those who love aromatic spices but don't like their food too hot.

chargrilled CHICKEN TIKKA

MARINADE

5 tbsp plain yogurt

2 tbsp tomato paste

2 tbsp lime or lemon juice

2 garlic cloves, finely chopped

1 tbsp grated fresh gingerroot

2 tsp ground cumin

2 tsp ground coriander

¼–½ tsp chili powder

pinch of garam masala

few drops of red food coloring
  (optional)

6 skinless, boneless chicken
  breasts, about 5 oz/140 g each

TO GARNISH

wedges of lemon

raw onion rings

pilau rice, to serve

SERVES 6

Mix together the yogurt, tomato paste, lime juice, garlic, ginger, cumin, coriander, chili powder, and garam masala in a large, shallow dish. Stir in a few drops of food coloring, if using.

Using a sharp knife, score the chicken 3–4 times and add to the dish, turning to coat. Cover with plastic wrap and let marinate in the refrigerator, turning occasionally, for 8 hours or overnight.

Grill the chicken for 20–30 minutes, or until tender and cooked through. Garnish with lemon wedges and onion rings, and serve at once with pilau rice.

spicy barbecued CHICKEN

A delicious tangy flavor is created by the lime juice in this sizzling recipe.

MARINADE

1½ tbsp chili oil

½ tsp brown sugar

½ tsp salt

1½ tsp ground allspice

1½ tsp dried mixed herbs

pepper

1½ tsp grated fresh gingerroot

4 shallots, chopped

6 scallions, finely chopped

4 garlic cloves, chopped

1 green chili and 1 red chili,
  seeded

CHICKEN

4 skinless, boneless chicken
  breasts, cut into slices

juice of 3 limes

scant 1 cup water

wedges of lime, to garnish

curly green lettuce leaves,
  to serve

SERVES 4

Put the chili oil, sugar, salt, allspice, and mixed herbs into a food processor
and season with plenty of black pepper. Blend well.

Add the grated ginger, shallots, scallions, and garlic. Finely chop the
chilies, add to the food processor and blend until fairly smooth. Transfer
to a glass bowl, cover with plastic wrap, and set aside.

Put the chicken slices into a nonmetallic (glass or ceramic) bowl, which will
not react with acid. Pour over the lime juice and water, then add enough
marinade to cover the chicken.

Cover with plastic wrap and let chill for at least 2½ hours. Cover the
remaining marinade with plastic wrap and let chill until the chicken is ready.

When the chicken slices are thoroughly marinated, lift them out, and
barbecue them over hot coals for 20–30 minutes, or until cooked right
through, turning them frequently and basting with the remaining marinade.
Serve on a bed of green lettuce leaves and garnish with lime wedges.

Lime juice combined with warm spices makes this a dish to remember.

chicken satay skewers
WITH LIME

MARINADE

generous ⅓ cup soy sauce

generous ⅓ cup lime juice

2 tbsp smooth peanut butter

2 tbsp garam masala

1 tbsp brown sugar

2 garlic cloves, finely chopped

1 small red chili, seeded and
    finely chopped

pepper

SKEWERS

6 skinless, boneless chicken
    breasts, cubed

TO GARNISH

fresh cilantro leaves, shredded
wedges of lime

freshly steamed or boiled rice,
    or crisp salad greens,
    to serve

SERVES 4

Put the soy sauce, lime juice, peanut butter, garam masala, sugar, garlic,
and chili into a large bowl and mix until well combined. Season with plenty
of pepper.

Thread the chicken cubes onto skewers (leave a small space at either end).
Transfer them to the bowl and turn them in the peanut butter mixture until
they are well coated. Cover with plastic wrap and place in the refrigerator to
marinate for at least 2½ hours.

When the skewers are thoroughly marinated, lift them out, and barbecue
them over hot coals for 15 minutes, or until cooked right through, turning
them frequently and basting with the remaining marinade. Arrange the
skewers on a bed of freshly cooked rice or crisp salad greens, garnish with
cilantro leaves and lime wedges, and serve.

moroccan CHICKEN

Allowing plenty of time for the chicken to marinate infuses it with the classic flavors of North Africa.

MARINADE

3 tbsp olive oil

4 tbsp lemon juice

2 tbsp chopped fresh parsley

2 tbsp chopped fresh cilantro

1 garlic clove, finely chopped

1 tsp ground coriander

½ tsp ground cumin

1 tsp sweet paprika

pinch of chili powder

4 skinless, boneless chicken
  breasts, about 5 oz/140 g each

TO SERVE

Carrot, Cabbage, and Mixed
  Fruit Salad (see page 145)

toasted flatbreads

SERVES 4

Mix together the oil, lemon juice, parsley, fresh cilantro, garlic,
ground coriander, cumin, paprika, and chili powder in a large, shallow,
nonmetallic dish.

Using a sharp knife, score the chicken breasts 3–4 times. Add the chicken to
the dish, turning to coat. Cover with plastic wrap and let marinate in a cool
place, turning occasionally, for 2–3 hours.

Drain the chicken, reserving the marinade. Grill, brushing occasionally with
the reserved marinade, for 20–30 minutes, or until tender and cooked
through. Season with salt and pepper and serve at once with the salad and
toasted flat breads.

This has a spicy authentic Asian flavor for the barbecue.

thai-style CHICKEN CHUNKS

MARINADE

1 red chili and 1 green chili,
   seeded and finely chopped
2 garlic cloves, chopped
1¾ oz/50 g chopped fresh
   cilantro
1 tbsp finely chopped fresh
   lemongrass
½ tsp ground turmeric
½ tsp garam masala
2 tsp brown sugar
2 tbsp Thai fish sauce
1 tbsp lime juice
salt and pepper

CHICKEN

4 skinless, boneless chicken
   breasts, cut into small chunks

chopped fresh cilantro,
   to garnish
freshly cooked jasmine rice,
   to serve

SERVES 4

Put the red and green chilies, garlic, cilantro, and lemongrass into a food processor and process until coarsely chopped. Add the turmeric, garam masala, sugar, fish sauce, and lime juice, season with salt and pepper, and blend until smooth.

Put the chicken chunks into a nonmetallic (glass or ceramic) bowl, which will not react with acid. Pour over enough marinade to cover the chicken, then cover with plastic wrap and let chill for at least 2¹/₂ hours. Cover the remaining marinade with plastic wrap and let chill until the chicken is ready.

When the chicken chunks are thoroughly marinated, lift them out, and barbecue them over hot coals for 20 minutes, or until cooked right through, turning them frequently and basting with the remaining marinade. Arrange the chicken on serving plates with some freshly cooked jasmine rice. Garnish with chopped fresh cilantro and serve.

chicken rolls WITH CHEESE

These tasty little rolls are guaranteed to be a barbecue favorite with adults and children alike.

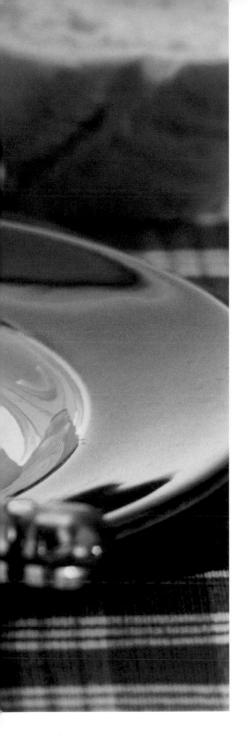

3 slices white bread, crusts
  removed
6 skinless, boneless chicken
  breasts, about 6 oz/175 g each
2 shallots, finely chopped
2 garlic cloves, finely chopped
2 tbsp finely chopped fresh
  flatleaf parsley

2 tbsp freshly grated Parmesan
  cheese
⅓ cup pine nuts
pinch of ground mace
tarragon-flavored oil or olive oil,
  for brushing
salt and pepper

few sprigs of fresh flatleaf
  parsley, to garnish

SERVES 6

Tear the bread into pieces, place in a bowl, and add cold water to cover.
Set aside to soak for 10 minutes.

Meanwhile, place the chicken breasts between 2 sheets of plastic wrap and
pound gently with a meat mallet or the side of a rolling pin to flatten.

Drain the bread and squeeze out the excess liquid. Mix together the bread,
shallots, garlic, parsley, Parmesan, pine nuts, and mace in a bowl. Season to
taste with salt and pepper.

Spread the filling evenly over the chicken breasts and roll up. Secure
each roll with a wooden toothpick. Brush with the oil and grill, turning
frequently and brushing with more oil as necessary, for 25–30 minutes, or
until cooked through and tender. Serve at once, garnished with parsley.

AND PINE NUTS

These chicken wings will soon become a family favorite.

sweet-and-sour
CHICKEN WINGS

MARINADE

2 tbsp sweet sherry

3 tbsp sherry vinegar or red
   wine vinegar

4 tbsp soy sauce

scant 1 cup orange juice

generous ⅓ cup chicken stock
   or vegetable stock

¼ cup brown sugar

pepper

1 tbsp tomato paste

2 garlic cloves, finely chopped

1 red chili, seeded and chopped

CHICKEN

4 lb/1.8 kg chicken wings

TO GARNISH

wedges of orange

1 long, red chili made into
   a flower

SERVES 4

Put the sherry, vinegar, soy sauce, orange juice, stock, and sugar into a food processor and season well. Blend until combined. Add the tomato paste, garlic, and chili and blend until smooth. Separate the chicken wings at the joints and put them into a nonmetallic (glass or ceramic) bowl, which will not react with acid. Pour over enough marinade to cover the chicken, cover with plastic wrap, and let chill for at least 2½ hours. Cover the remaining marinade with plastic wrap and let chill until the chicken is ready.

When the chicken wings are thoroughly marinated, lift them out, and barbecue them over hot coals for about 20 minutes, turning them frequently and basting with the remaining marinade. Cut into a thick part of a wing to check that the chicken is cooked all the way through. If it is still pink in the center, continue to cook until the chicken is thoroughly cooked. Garnish with orange wedges and a chili flower (made by making ½-inch/1-cm slits in a chili and soaking in iced water for 30 minutes until fanned out).

chicken TERIYAKI

This Japanese-style marinade gives a wonderful flavor and attractive color to the chicken.

MARINADE

1 tbsp cornstarch

½ cup dark soy sauce

4 tbsp rice wine or dry sherry

2 tbsp rice or white wine vinegar

2 tbsp clear honey

4 x 5 oz/140 g skinless, boneless
   chicken breasts

fresh garlic chives, to garnish

mixed salad greens, to serve

SERVES 4

Put the cornstarch and soy sauce in a bowl and mix to a smooth paste. Stir in the rice wine, vinegar, and honey until thoroughly combined. Pour three-quarters of this mixture into a large, shallow dish and reserve the remainder.

Using a sharp knife, score the chicken 3–4 times and add to the dish, turning to coat. Cover with plastic wrap and let marinate in a cool place, turning occasionally, for 2–3 hours.

Pour the reserved marinade into a small pan and heat, stirring constantly, until slightly thickened. Transfer the pan to the side of the barbecue to keep warm.

Drain the chicken, reserving the marinade. Grill, brushing frequently with the reserved marinade, for 5–8 minutes on each side, or until cooked through and tender.

Place the chicken on a bed of mixed salad greens on 4 serving plates. Spoon over the hot marinade from the pan, garnish with garlic chives, and serve at once.

The flavors and aromas of the Mediterranean turn a simple piece of chicken into a summer feast.

pesto and ricotta CHICKEN

1 tbsp pesto sauce

½ cup ricotta cheese

4 x 6 oz/175 g skinless, boneless
  chicken breasts

1 tbsp olive oil

pepper

small salad, to garnish

TOMATO VINAIGRETTE

generous ⅓ cup olive oil

1 bunch fresh chives

1 lb 2 oz/500 g tomatoes, peeled,
  seeded, and chopped

juice and finely grated rind of
  1 lime

salt and pepper

SERVES 4

Mix together the pesto and ricotta in a small bowl until well combined. Using
a sharp knife, cut a deep slit in the side of each chicken breast to make a
pocket. Spoon the ricotta mixture into the pockets and reshape the chicken
breasts to enclose it. Place the chicken on a plate, cover, and let chill for
30 minutes.

To make the vinaigrette, pour the olive oil into a blender or food processor,
add the chives, and process until smooth. Scrape the mixture into a bowl
and stir in the tomatoes, lime juice, and rind. Season to taste with salt
and pepper.

Brush the chicken with the olive oil and season with pepper. Grill on a fairly
hot barbecue for about 8 minutes on each side, or until cooked through and
tender. Transfer to serving plates, spoon over the vinaigrette, and serve
at once.

sherried chicken
AND MUSHROOM KABOBS

The inclusion of sherry makes this quite a special dish for a party.

MARINADE

¼ cup soy sauce

2 tbsp sweet sherry

¼ cup vegetable oil

1 tsp brown sugar

1 tbsp honey

1 garlic clove, finely chopped

pepper

KABOBS

6 skinless, boneless chicken
    breasts, cubed

16 white mushrooms

16 pearl onions

16 cherry tomatoes

fresh flatleaf parsley,
    to garnish

freshly steamed or boiled rice,
    to serve

SERVES 4

Put the soy sauce, sweet sherry, oil, sugar, and honey into a large bowl.
Add the garlic and mix until well combined. Season with plenty of pepper.

Thread the chicken cubes onto 8 skewers, alternating them with the
mushrooms, onions, and cherry tomatoes. When the skewers are full (leave
a small space at either end), transfer them to the bowl, and turn them in the
sherry mixture until they are well coated. Cover with plastic wrap and place
in the refrigerator to marinate for at least 2½ hours.

When the kabobs are thoroughly marinated, lift them out, and barbecue
them over hot coals for 15–20 minutes, or until cooked right through, turning
them frequently and basting with the remaining marinade. Arrange the
kabobs on a bed of freshly cooked rice, garnish with fresh flatleaf parsley,
and serve.

Flattening out these little chickens isn't difficult and ensures that they cook through evenly.

spatchcocked
SQUAB CHICKEN

4 oz/115 g unsalted butter,
  softened
2 tbsp tarragon mustard
1 tbsp finely chopped fresh
  tarragon
1 small onion, chopped
finely grated rind and juice
  of 1 lemon
4 squab chickens, about 1 lb/
  450 g each
olive oil, for brushing
salt and pepper

SERVES 4

Place the butter, mustard, chopped tarragon, onion, and lemon rind and juice in a blender or food processor and process until smooth. Scrape into a bowl and set aside.

Using poultry shears, cut the squab chickens along each side of the backbone and remove and discard it. Place each bird flat on a cutting board, cut-side down, and press firmly on the breastbone with the heel of your hand to flatten.

Carefully lift the skin over the breast of each bird and gently push your fingers between the flesh and skin to make a pocket. Spread the flavored butter under the skin and gently smooth back in place.

Thread a skewer through a drumstick, under the breastbone, and through the second drumstick of each bird. Thread another skewer through the wings. Brush the birds with the oil and grill on a medium-hot barbecue, turning occasionally, for 15–20 minutes, or until cooked through and tender. Serve at once.

duck breasts
WITH CAESAR SALAD

This is a marriage made in heaven—the richness of the duck is complemented by the refreshing salad.

1 tbsp coriander seeds

10 juniper berries

1 tsp green peppercorns

6 dried bay leaves, crumbled

1 lb 2 oz/500 g boneless duck
   breasts

1 tbsp orange juice

1 tbsp olive oil

salt and pepper

CAESAR SALAD

4 canned anchovies, chopped

6 tbsp lemon juice

2 garlic cloves, chopped

2 tsp Dijon mustard

1 large egg yolk

1¼ cups olive oil

1 large romaine lettuce, torn
   into pieces

4 tbsp freshly grated Parmesan
   cheese

4 slices of bread, cubed and
   cooked until crisp

SERVES 6

Put the coriander seeds, juniper berries, peppercorns, and bay leaves into a mortar and add ½ tsp salt. Grind to a powder. Rub the duck breasts all over with the spice mixture. Place in a dish, cover, and let marinate in the refrigerator overnight.

An hour before you are ready to cook, remove the duck from the refrigerator, and wipe off most of the spice mix with paper towels. Whisk together the orange juice and olive oil in a small bowl and set aside.

Meanwhile, prepare the salad. Put the anchovies, lemon juice, garlic, mustard, and egg yolk in a blender or food processor and process until smooth. With the machine running, gradually trickle in the olive oil until the dressing emulsifies. Season to taste. Place the lettuce in a bowl, add half the dressing, and 3 tbsp of the Parmesan. Toss well.

Brush the duck breasts with the orange juice mixture and grill, skin-side down, for 5 minutes. Turn, brush with more juice mixture and grill for 10–12 minutes, or until cooked to your liking. Let rest for 2–3 minutes, then slice into strips.

Divide the lettuce between 6 plates, sprinkle with the bread cubes, and top with the duck. Drizzle over the remaining dressing, sprinkle with the remaining Parmesan, and serve.

The slight sharpness of the relish contrasts delightfully with the sweet glaze and rich meat.

duck breasts WITH MAPLE

SERVES 4

For the relish, put the cranberries, shallots, wine, and sugar into a pan and bring to a boil, stirring. Reduce the heat and let simmer for 10–15 minutes, until soft. Mix together the cornstarch, orange juice, and allspice in a small bowl, then stir into the cranberries. Add the orange rind and cook, stirring, until thickened. Remove from the heat, cover, and let cool, then let chill until ready to serve.

Cut off any excess fat from the duck breasts and score the skin. Cut the duck breasts into 1-inch/2.5-cm cubes and thread onto skewers. Mix together the maple syrup, orange juice and rind, and lemon juice and rind in a bowl.

Grill the duck breasts for 2 minutes on each side, then brush with the maple syrup mixture. Grill, turning and brushing with the maple syrup mixture frequently, for about 8 minutes, or until cooked through and tender. Serve at once, with the cranberry relish.

4 duck breasts, about 8 oz/
  225 g each
4 tbsp maple syrup
juice and finely grated rind
  of 1 orange
juice and finely grated rind
  of 1 lemon

CRANBERRY RELISH
2 cups fresh or frozen
  cranberries
2 shallots, finely chopped
⅔ cup red wine
generous ½ cup superfine sugar
2 tsp cornstarch
juice and finely grated rind
  of 1 orange
1 tsp ground allspice

turkey scallops WITH A

This recipe is simplicity itself and cooks very quickly so it is ideal if you have a lot of hungry guests.

4–6 tbsp dry, undyed
   bread crumbs
4–6 tbsp freshly grated
   Parmesan cheese
½ tsp chopped fresh sage
pepper
4 turkey scallops,
   about 5 oz/140 g each
2 tbsp olive oil

TO GARNISH
orange and lemon slices
sprig of fresh sage

SERVES 4

Mix together the bread crumbs, Parmesan, and sage in a bowl and season
with pepper.

Place the turkey scallops between 2 sheets of plastic wrap and pound
gently with a meat mallet or the side of a rolling pin to flatten to about
¼ inch/5 mm thick.

Brush the turkey on both sides with half the olive oil, then sprinkle with the
bread crumb mixture, pressing it on with your hands to coat completely.

Grill for 2–3 minutes on each side, or until cooked through and the crust is
crisp. Serve at once, sprinkled with the remaining olive oil, and garnished
with orange and lemon slices and a sprig of sage.

PARMESAN CRUST

Marinating the chops with gherkins and capers gives them a delightfully piquant flavor.

italian marinated
PORK CHOPS

4 pork rib chops

4 fresh sage leaves

2 tbsp salted capers

2 gherkins, chopped

small salad, to garnish

garlic bread (optional), to serve

MARINADE

4 tbsp dry white wine

1 tbsp brown sugar

2 tbsp olive oil

1 tsp Dijon mustard

SERVES 4

Trim any visible fat from the chops and place them in a large, shallow dish. Top each with a sage leaf. Rub the salt off the capers with your fingers and sprinkle them over the chops, together with the gherkins.

Mix the wine, sugar, oil, and mustard together in a small bowl and pour the mixture over the chops. Cover with plastic wrap and let marinate in a cool place for about 2 hours.

Drain the chops, reserving the marinade. Grill the chops on a hot barbecue for 5 minutes on each side, then grill over more medium coals or on a higher rack, turning and brushing occasionally with the reserved marinade, for about 10 minutes more on each side, or until cooked through and tender. Serve at once with a small salad and garlic bread if you like.

pork steaks
WITH MUSTARD AND APPLE

This is a classic partnership—the mustard and apple are combined into a tasty topping.

2 eating apples, peeled, cored,
  and grated
1 cup fresh whole-wheat bread
  crumbs
1 tbsp chopped fresh sage
2 tsp whole-grain mustard
4 pork steaks
olive oil, for brushing

TO GARNISH
wedges of lemon
small salad

SERVES 4

Mix together the grated apples, bread crumbs, sage, and mustard in a bowl.
Trim any visible fat from the pork steaks and brush with oil.

Grill the pork steaks over a medium barbecue for 6–7 minutes. Remove the
steaks from the barbecue, transfer to a board, and turn them over. Press the
topping firmly over them, then grill for an additional 10–15 minutes.

Carefully transfer the steaks to serving plates, topping-side up, garnish with
lemon wedges and a small salad, and serve at once.

Rather like sweet-and-sour pork with a hint of citrus.

tangy PORK RIBS

SERVES 4

Preheat the oven to 475°F/240°C. Combine the salt, paprika, and pepper in a baking dish and then add the ribs. Turn them in the dish to coat them well all over. Cook in the center of the preheated oven for 1¾–2 hours, then remove the dish from the oven, lift out the ribs, drain off the fat and set aside.

Heat the oil in a skillet. Add the onion, scallions, garlic, ginger, and chili and stir-fry over high heat for 1 minute. Then add the herbs, sherry, sugar, chili bean sauce, tomato paste, rice wine, vinegar, orange juice, and soy sauce. Stir in a large pinch of salt and season well with pepper. Bring to a boil, reduce the heat, and let simmer for 15–20 minutes, stirring occasionally. To barbecue the ribs, coat them in the sauce, then grill them over hot coals for 7–10 minutes on each side, or until cooked right through, turning them frequently and basting with more sauce as necessary. Serve at once, accompanied by orange wedges.

1¼ tsp salt

2 tsp paprika

2 tsp pepper

3 lb/1.3 kg pork ribs

1 tbsp chili or vegetable oil

1 onion, finely chopped

6 scallions, chopped

3 garlic cloves, chopped

2 tsp finely chopped fresh
  gingerroot

1 red chili, chopped

1 tbsp chopped fresh cilantro

1 tbsp chopped flatleaf parsley

1 tbsp sweet sherry

1½ tbsp brown sugar

4 tbsp Chinese chili bean sauce

1 tbsp tomato paste

1 tbsp rice wine

1 tbsp sherry vinegar

generous ⅓ cup orange juice

2½ tbsp soy sauce

salt and pepper

wedges of orange, to serve

herbed pork chops

The flavored butter adds a wonderfully rich taste to the barbecued chops as it melts.

4 pork chops

MARINADE

4 tbsp corn oil

2 tbsp lemon juice

1 tbsp chopped fresh marjoram

1 tbsp chopped fresh thyme

2 tablespoons chopped fresh
  parsley

1 garlic clove, finely chopped

1 onion, finely chopped

salt and pepper

small salad, to serve

BLUE CHEESE &
WALNUT BUTTER

2 oz/55 g butter

4 scallions, finely chopped

5 oz/140 g Gorgonzola cheese,
  crumbled

2 tbsp finely chopped walnuts

SERVES 4

Trim the fat from the chops and place them in a dish. Whisk together the oil, lemon juice, marjoram, thyme, parsley, garlic, and onion in a bowl, then season with salt and pepper. Pour the marinade over the chops, turning to coat. Cover and let marinate in the refrigerator overnight.

To make the flavored butter, melt half the butter in a skillet, and cook the scallions over low heat, stirring frequently for a few minutes, until softened. Transfer to a bowl and mix in the remaining butter, the cheese, and walnuts. Form into a roll, then cover and let chill until required.

Drain the chops, reserving the marinade. Grill the chops on a hot barbecue for 5 minutes on each side, then grill over more medium coals or on a higher rack, turning and brushing occasionally with the reserved marinade, for about 10 minutes more on each side, or until cooked through and tender. Transfer to serving plates and top each chop with 1–2 slices of the cheese and walnut butter. Serve at once with a small salad.

WITH BLUE CHEESE AND WALNUT BUTTER

Fruit counterbalances the richness of the pork in this recipe.

pork and prune KABOBS

1 lb 2 oz/500 g pork fillet, cut into
   1-inch/2.5-cm cubes
36 prunes, pitted

MARINADE
6 tbsp olive oil
6 tbsp Calvados or applejack
1 tbsp chopped fresh oregano

36 pearl onions, peeled
salt and pepper

APPLE CREAM
2 eating apples, peeled, cored,
   and coarsely chopped
1 tbsp honey
⅔ cup apple juice
1 tbsp Calvados or applejack
1 tbsp corn oil
3 tbsp cider vinegar
⅔ cup sour cream

SERVES 6

Place the pork cubes and prunes in a shallow dish. Mix together the olive oil, Calvados, and oregano in a bowl, pour over the meat, and stir well. Cover with plastic wrap and let marinate in the refrigerator overnight.

To make the apple cream, put the apples in a food processor and process to a coarse purée. Add all the remaining ingredients and process to combine. Scrape into a bowl, cover, and let chill until required.

Drain the meat and prunes, reserving the marinade. Thread the pork, prunes, and pearl onions alternately onto skewers. Grill the kabobs on a medium barbecue, turning and brushing occasionally with the reserved marinade, for 10–12 minutes. Season with salt and pepper and serve with the apple cream.

pork medallions
WITH GRILLED APPLES

This tasty chargrilled treat needs to be served with no more than a mixed salad and some crusty bread.

1 lb 2 oz/500 g pork fillet

4 eating apples, cored

4 small rosemary sprigs, plus
   extra to garnish

4 tsp superfine sugar

MARINADE

2 tbsp olive oil

1 garlic clove, finely chopped

4 shallots, finely chopped

4 tbsp orange juice

2 tbsp honey

1 tbsp Worcestershire sauce

1 tsp Dijon mustard

3 tbsp white wine vinegar

1 rosemary sprig, finely chopped

SERVES 4

Make the marinade. Heat the oil and cook the garlic and shallots over low heat, stirring occasionally, for 5 minutes, until soft. Stir in the remaining marinade ingredients and let simmer gently for 5 minutes. Remove from the heat and let cool completely.

Cut the pork fillet into medallions about 1/2 inch/1 cm thick and place in a shallow dish. Pour in the marinade, turning to coat. Cover with plastic wrap and let marinate in the refrigerator overnight.

With a sharp knife, score through the skin of each apple around the center. Place each apple on a square of foil and put a rosemary sprig and 1 tsp sugar in each cavity. Enclose the apples in the foil and cook on a medium barbecue, turning occasionally, for 25–30 minutes.

About 10–15 minutes before the apples are ready, drain the pork, reserving the marinade. Grill, brushing with the reserved marinade for about 5 minutes on each side. Put 3–4 medallions on each plate with an unwrapped apple. Garnish with extra rosemary sprigs and serve.

These colorful skewers look inviting and are perfect for an outdoor party.

cherry tomato, ham, and

1 tbsp vegetable oil

1 tbsp white wine vinegar

1 tsp mustard powder

1 tbsp clear honey

1 lb/450 g cooked ham steak,
   cubed

1 lb/450 g canned pineapple
   chunks, drained

12 cherry tomatoes

freshly cooked rice, fresh green
   lettuce leaves, or crusty bread,
   to serve

SERVES 4

Put the oil, vinegar, mustard powder, and honey into a bowl and mix until
well combined.

Thread the ham onto skewers, alternating it with pineapple chunks and
whole cherry tomatoes. When the skewers are full (leave a small space at
either end), brush them with the honey mixture until they are well coated.

Barbecue the skewers over hot coals, turning them frequently, for about
10 minutes, or until cooked right through. Serve them with freshly boiled rice,
fresh green lettuce leaves, or crusty bread.

pineapple SKEWERS

barbecued
PORK SAUSAGES WITH THYME

Homemade sausages are made even more tempting with these tasty ingredients.

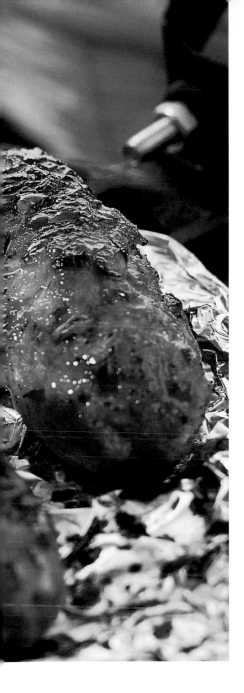

1 garlic clove, finely chopped

1 onion, grated

1 small red chili, seeded and
    finely chopped

1 lb/450 g lean ground pork

scant ⅔ cup almonds, toasted
    and ground

⅞ cup fresh bread crumbs

1 tbsp finely chopped
    fresh thyme

salt and pepper

flour, for dusting

vegetable oil, for brushing

TO SERVE

fresh hotdog rolls

slices of onion, lightly cooked

tomato ketchup and/or mustard

SERVES 4

Put the garlic, onion, chili, pork, almonds, bread crumbs, and thyme into a large bowl. Season well with salt and pepper and mix until well combined.

Using your hands, form the mixture into sausage shapes. Roll each sausage in a little flour, then transfer to a bowl, cover with plastic wrap, and let chill for 45 minutes.

Brush a piece of aluminum foil with oil, then put the sausages on the foil and brush them with a little more vegetable oil. Transfer the sausages and foil to the barbecue.

Barbecue over hot coals, turning the sausages frequently, for about 15 minutes, or until cooked right through. Serve with hotdog rolls, cooked sliced onion, and tomato ketchup and/or mustard.

This is a wonderfully messy meal that everyone loves, perfect for eating outdoors.

sweet-and-sour RIBS

4 scallions, finely chopped

3 tbsp lemon juice

⅔ cup white wine vinegar

2 tsp English mustard

3 tbsp brown sugar

3 tbsp Worcestershire sauce

5 tbsp sundried tomato paste

2 lb 4 oz/1 kg pork spareribs

salt and pepper

SERVES 4

Put the scallions, lemon juice, vinegar, mustard, sugar, Worcestershire sauce, and sundried tomato paste in a pan, season with salt and pepper, and bring to a boil, stirring well to mix. Reduce the heat and let simmer, stirring occasionally, for 30 minutes. Transfer the pan to the side of the barbecue.

Using a sharp knife, make deep scores all over the racks of ribs, then brush them all over with the sauce.

Grill over a medium barbecue, turning and brushing frequently with the sauce, for 1–1¼ hours, or until cooked through and tender. Serve at once.

curried lamb SKEWERS

A subtle combination of flavors makes this a stylish dish for a barbecue.

MARINADE

2 tsp vegetable oil

1 tsp curry powder

1 tsp garam masala

2 tsp granulated sugar

scant 1 cup plain yogurt

SKEWERS

14 oz/400 g boneless lamb,
  cubed

scant 1 cup dried apricot halves

1 red or green bell pepper,
  seeded and cut into
  small chunks

2 zucchini, cubed

16 pearl onions

fresh cilantro leaves, to garnish

TO SERVE

freshly steamed or boiled rice

crisp salad greens

SERVES 4

Put the oil, spices, sugar, and yogurt into a large bowl and mix until
well combined.

Thread the lamb onto 8 skewers, alternating it with the apricot halves, red
bell pepper, zucchini, and pearl onions. When the skewers are full (leave a
small space at either end), transfer them to the bowl, and turn them in the
yogurt mixture until they are well coated. Cover with plastic wrap and place
in the refrigerator to marinate for at least 8 hours or overnight.

When the skewers are thoroughly marinated, lift them out, and barbecue
them over hot coals, turning them frequently, for 15 minutes, or until the
meat is cooked right through. Serve at once with freshly cooked rice or crisp
salad greens, garnished with fresh cilantro leaves.

The earthy flavor of wild mushrooms goes well with the sweetness of lamb.

lamb and wild mushroom BROCHETTES

½ cup red wine

6 tbsp olive oil

1 tbsp lemon juice

salt and pepper

1 large onion, chopped

2 garlic cloves, finely chopped

1 tbsp chopped fresh thyme

2 lb 4 oz/1 kg boned leg of lamb,
   cut into 1-inch/2.5-cm cubes

12 slices lean bacon, rinds
   removed

24 wild mushrooms

6 cherry tomatoes

rice salad, to serve

rosemary sprigs and chopped
   fresh thyme, to garnish

SERVES 6

Pour the wine, olive oil, and lemon juice into a large, shallow dish and season with salt and pepper. Stir in the onion, garlic, and thyme, then add the lamb and stir again to coat. Cover with plastic wrap and let marinate in the refrigerator for 4 hours.

Drain the lamb, reserving the marinade. Loosely roll up the bacon slices. Thread the cubes of lamb, bacon rolls, and mushrooms alternately onto 6 long skewers and finish each with a cherry tomato.

Brush the brochettes generously with the reserved marinade. Grill on a medium barbecue, turning and brushing occasionally with the marinade, for about 15 minutes, or until cooked through and tender. Serve at once, with a rice salad.

spicy rack of lamb
WITH HUMMUS

The lamb in this dish is partly cooked before marinating and then browned on the barbecue.

6 racks of lamb, each
   with 3 chops
2 tbsp olive oil

MARINADE

1 tbsp olive oil

2 tbsp honey

2 tsp ground coriander

2 tsp ground cumin

1 tsp ground allspice

½ tsp paprika

few sprigs of fresh mint,
   to garnish
hummus, to serve

SERVES 6

Preheat the oven to 375°F/190°C. Put the lamb in a roasting pan and
spoon over 2 tbsp of olive oil. Roast for 10–15 minutes, or until almost
cooked through.

Mix together 1 tbsp of olive oil, the honey, coriander, cumin, allspice, and
paprika in a small bowl. Brush the spice mixture all over the warm lamb, then
place in a dish and let cool. Cover with plastic wrap and let marinate in the
refrigerator overnight.

Cook the lamb on a medium barbecue, turning frequently, until heated
through and well browned. Transfer to 6 serving plates, add 2–3 tbsp hummus
to each, garnish with mint sprigs, and serve.

Balsamic vinegar has a wonderfully rich and mellow flavor, while rosemary is traditional with lamb.

lamb with balsamic
and ROSEMARY MARINADE

6 racks of lamb, each with
  3 chops

MARINADE

3 tbsp chopped fresh rosemary

1 small onion, finely chopped

3 tbsp olive oil

1 tbsp balsamic vinegar

1 tbsp lemon juice

salt and pepper

fresh rosemary sprigs, to garnish

SERVES 6

Put the lamb in a large, shallow dish and sprinkle with the chopped rosemary and onion. Whisk together the olive oil, balsamic vinegar, and lemon juice and season with salt and pepper.

Pour the balsamic mixture over the lamb, turning well to coat. Cover with plastic wrap and set aside in a cool place to marinate for 1–2 hours.

Drain the lamb, reserving the marinade. Grill the racks, brushing frequently with the reserved marinade, for 8–10 minutes on each side. Serve garnished with rosemary sprigs.

greek-style beef KABOBS

Your barbecue party takes on a Greek theme with these tasty kabobs.

1 small onion, finely chopped

1 tbsp chopped fresh cilantro

large pinch of paprika

¼ tsp ground allspice

¼ tsp ground coriander

¼ tsp brown sugar

1 lb/450 g ground beef

salt and pepper

vegetable oil, for brushing

fresh cilantro leaves, to garnish

TO SERVE

freshly cooked bulgur wheat or rice

mixed salad

SERVES 4

Put the onion, fresh cilantro, spices, sugar, and beef into a large bowl and mix until well combined. Season with salt and pepper.

On a clean counter, use your hands to shape the mixture into sausages around skewers. Brush them lightly with vegetable oil.

Barbecue the kabobs over hot coals, turning them frequently, for 15–20 minutes, or until cooked right through. Arrange the kabobs on a platter of freshly cooked bulgur wheat or rice and garnish with fresh cilantro leaves. Serve with a mixed salad.

An aristocratic relation of the humble burger, this is a positive feast for serious meateaters.

new orleans steak
SANDWICH

4 tbsp olive oil

2 large onions, sliced thinly into rings

2 garlic cloves, chopped

1 tbsp red wine vinegar

1 tbsp chopped fresh thyme

3 tbsp chopped fresh parsley

2 tsp prepared mild mustard

salt and pepper

4 rump steaks, about 6 oz/ 175 g each

8 slices sourdough or crusty bread

4 oz/115 g Roquefort cheese, crumbled

4 tomatoes, sliced

1 Boston lettuce, shredded

SERVES 4

Heat half the oil in a heavy-bottom skillet. Add the onions and garlic, sprinkle with a pinch of salt, then cover and cook over very low heat for 25–30 minutes, or until very soft and caramelized.

Process the onion mixture in a food processor until smooth. Scrape into a bowl, stir in the vinegar, thyme, parsley, and mustard and season with salt and pepper. Cover and place at the side of the barbecue.

Brush the steaks with the remaining oil and season with salt and pepper. Grill on a hot barbecue for 2 minutes on each side for rare, 4 minutes on each side for medium, or 6 minutes on each side for well done.

Meanwhile, toast the bread on both sides. Spread the onion mixture on the toast. Slice the steaks and top 4 toast slices with the meat. Sprinkle with the crumbled Roquefort, then add the tomatoes and lettuce leaves. Top with the remaining toast and serve.

sozzled SIRLOIN

Although beer is used in a wide range of beef stews, it rarely features in barbecue marinades—until now.

6 sirloin steaks, about 6 oz/
    175 g each

MARINADE

¾ cup Guinness

2 tbsp corn oil

3 tbsp brown sugar

2 tbsp Worcestershire sauce

1 tbsp whole-grain mustard

MUSTARD BUTTER

2 garlic cloves, finely chopped

8 oz/225 g butter, softened

2 tbsp tarragon mustard

1 tbsp chopped fresh parsley

SERVES 6

Place the steaks in a large, shallow dish. Mix together the Guinness, corn oil, sugar, Worcestershire sauce, whole-grain mustard, and garlic in a pitcher. Pour the mixture over the steaks, turning to coat. Cover with plastic wrap and let marinate in the refrigerator for 4 hours.

Meanwhile, beat together the butter, mustard, and parsley in a bowl until combined. Cover and let chill until required.

Drain the steaks, reserving the marinade. Grill on a hot barbecue, brushing frequently with the marinade, for 2 minutes on each side for rare, 4 minutes on each side for medium, or 6 minutes on each side for well done. Serve at once, topped with the mustard butter.

This barbecue favorite is marinated in a spicy sauce and served with a topping of shallot butter.

rump steak WITH DARK BARBECUE SAUCE

2 tbsp corn oil

MARINADE

1 onion, finely chopped

1 lb/450 g tomatoes, peeled, seeded, and chopped

2 tbsp lemon juice

1 tbsp Tabasco sauce

2 tbsp Worcestershire sauce

2 tbsp brown sugar

1 tsp mustard powder

5 oz/140 g shallots, finely chopped

5 oz/140 g butter, softened

6 rump steaks, about 6 oz/ 175 g each

salt and pepper

few sprigs of watercress, to garnish

SERVES 6

Heat the oil in a large skillet. Cook the onion over low heat, stirring occasionally, for 5 minutes, or until softened. Stir in the tomatoes, lemon juice, Tabasco and Worcestershire sauces, sugar, and mustard powder. Cover and let simmer, stirring occasionally, for 15–20 minutes, or until thickened. Pour into a large dish and let cool.

Meanwhile, blanch the shallots in boiling water for 2–3 minutes. Drain well and pat dry with paper towels. Place in a food processor and process to a purée. Gradually work in the butter and season with salt and pepper. Scrape the shallot butter into a bowl, cover, and let chill until required.

Add the steaks to the cooled marinade, turning to coat. Cover and let marinate in a cool place for 4 hours.

Drain the steaks, reserving the marinade. Grill on a hot barbecue, brushing frequently with the marinade, for 2 minutes on each side for rare, 4 minutes on each side for medium, or 6 minutes on each side for well done. Serve each steak topped with a spoonful of shallot butter and garnish with watercress sprigs.

steak WITH BLUE CHEESE TOPPING

A tangy topping makes all the difference between a routine meal and a special barbecue treat.

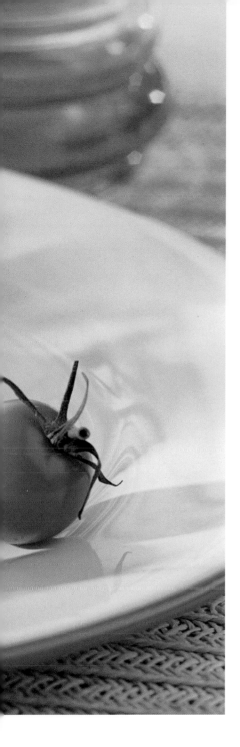

MARINADE

⅔ cup red wine

1 tbsp red wine vinegar

1 tbsp olive oil

1 garlic clove, finely chopped

1 bay leaf, crumbled

1 tbsp whole-grain mustard

4 rump or sirloin steaks, about
6 oz/175 g each

2 oz/55 g blue cheese, such
as Gorgonzola

1 cup fresh white bread crumbs

2 tbsp chopped fresh parsley

small salad, to garnish

SERVES 4

Mix together the red wine, vinegar, olive oil, garlic, bay leaf, and mustard in a shallow dish. Add the steaks, turning to coat, then cover and let stand in a cool place to marinate for 4 hours.

Meanwhile, mix together the blue cheese, bread crumbs, and parsley in a small bowl. Cover and store in the refrigerator until required.

Drain the steaks. Grill for 2 minutes on each side for rare, 4 minutes on each side for medium, or 6 minutes on each side for well done. Spoon the cheese topping onto the steaks, pressing it down with the back of the spoon, when you turn the steaks. Serve at once, garnished with a small salad.

A spicy, flavorsome treat for a special barbecue.

thai-spiced beef
AND BELL PEPPER KABOBS

SERVES 4

Put the sherry, rice wine, soy sauce, hoisin sauce, garlic, chili, ginger, and scallions into a large bowl and mix until well combined. Season to taste.

Thread the meat onto 8 skewers, alternating it with chunks of red bell pepper. When the skewers are full (leave a small space at either end), transfer them to the bowl, and turn them in the soy sauce mixture until they are well coated. Cover with plastic wrap and place in the refrigerator to marinate for at least 2½ hours or overnight.

When the skewers are thoroughly marinated, lift them out, and barbecue them over hot coals, turning them frequently, for 10–15 minutes, or until the meat is cooked right through. Serve at once on a bed of green and red lettuce leaves.

MARINADE

2 tbsp sherry

2 tbsp rice wine

generous ¼ cup soy sauce

generous ¼ cup hoisin sauce

3 garlic cloves, finely chopped

1 red chili, seeded and
    finely chopped

1½ tbsp grated fresh gingerroot

3 scallions, finely chopped

salt and pepper

KABOBS

2 lb 4 oz/1 kg rump or sirloin
    steak, cubed

2 large red bell peppers, seeded
    and cut into small chunks

green and red lettuce leaves,
    to serve

spicy thai-style BURGERS

Burgers with added spice make an everyday dish a little special.

⅜ cup fresh bread crumbs, white
   or whole-wheat
1½ tbsp finely chopped scallions
1 garlic clove, finely chopped
1½ tbsp chopped fresh
   lemongrass
1½ tbsp chopped fresh cilantro
2 tsp almonds, chopped
2 tsp peanuts, chopped
1 lb 2 oz/500 g ground beef
1 small red chili, seeded and
   finely chopped
salt and pepper

TO SERVE
hamburger buns
wedges of lemon and lime
shredded fresh napa cabbage

SERVES 4

Put the bread crumbs, scallions, garlic, lemongrass, cilantro, nuts, beef, and chili into a large bowl and mix until well combined. Season with salt and pepper.

Using your hands, form the mixture into burger shapes. Barbecue the burgers over hot coals for 5–8 minutes on each side, or until cooked right through. Serve in hamburger buns with wedges of lemon and lime and shredded napa cabbage.

This is a terrific meal for children—irresistible homemade burgers they can assemble themselves.

classic burger IN A BUN

2 lb 4 oz/1 kg lean steak, ground
1 cup fresh bread crumbs
1 egg, lightly beaten
1 tbsp chopped fresh thyme
salt and pepper

TO SERVE
6 burger buns
lettuce leaves
red onion slices
tomato slices
dill pickle slices (optional)
tomato ketchup, relishes,
    mustard of choice

SERVES 6

Put the ground steak, bread crumbs, egg, and thyme in a bowl and season
with salt and pepper. Mix thoroughly, using your hands.

Divide the mixture into 6 portions and shape each into a circle. Place on a
plate, cover, and let chill for 30 minutes to firm up.

Cook the burgers over a medium barbecue for 3–5 minutes on each side,
depending on how well done you like them. Turn them carefully as they will
not be as firm as store-bought burgers. Split the burger buns and toast them,
cut-side down, until golden. Place a burger in each bun and serve with a
selection of fillings and accompaniments (well away from the barbecue fire).

beefburgers
WITH CHILI AND BASIL

A tasty traditional barbecue dish—with an extra spiciness.

1 lb 7 oz/650 g ground beef
1 red bell pepper, seeded and
finely chopped
1 garlic clove, finely chopped
2 small red chilies, seeded and
finely chopped
1 tbsp chopped fresh basil
½ tsp ground cumin
salt and pepper

sprigs of fresh basil, to garnish
hamburger buns, to serve

SERVES 4

Put the ground beef, red bell pepper, garlic, chilies, chopped basil, and
cumin into a bowl and mix until well combined. Season with salt and pepper.

Using your hands, form the mixture into burger shapes. Barbecue the
burgers over hot coals for 5–8 minutes on each side, or until cooked right
through. Garnish with sprigs of basil and serve in hamburger buns.

fish AND seafood

Rich in vitamins and minerals, fish provides a nutritious alternative to poultry and meat and is tasty cooked on the barbecue. In this section you will find a number of delicious and unusual recipes that use a variety of fresh fish and are very easy to prepare and cook. These recipes, using inventive ingredients and accompaniments from different parts of the world, will enable you to cook barbecued fish dishes with confidence.

Delicate flavors make these shrimp a real barbecue treat.

asian shrimp SKEWERS

MARINADE

generous ⅓ cup vegetable oil

2 tbsp chili oil

¼ cup lemon juice

1 tbsp rice wine or sherry

2 scallions, finely chopped

2 garlic cloves, finely chopped

1 tbsp grated fresh gingerroot

1 tbsp chopped fresh
    lemongrass

2 tbsp chopped fresh cilantro

salt and pepper

SKEWERS

2 lb 4 oz/1 kg large shrimp,
    shelled and deveined, but with
    tails left on

TO GARNISH

wedges of lemon

chopped fresh chives

freshly cooked jasmine rice,
    to serve

SERVES 4

Put the oils, lemon juice, rice wine, scallions, garlic, ginger, lemongrass, and cilantro into a food processor and season well with salt and pepper. Process until smooth, then transfer to a nonmetallic (glass or ceramic) bowl, which will not react with acid.

Add the shrimp to the bowl and turn them in the mixture until they are well coated. Cover with plastic wrap and place in the refrigerator to marinate for at least 2 hours.

When the shrimp are thoroughly marinated, lift them out, and thread them onto skewers, leaving a small space at either end. Barbecue them with the lemon wedges over hot coals for 4–5 minutes, or until cooked right through (but do not overcook), turning them frequently and basting with the remaining marinade. Arrange the skewers on a bed of freshly cooked jasmine rice. Garnish with the lemon wedges and chopped fresh chives.

shrimp IN COCONUT MILK AND

Give your barbecue an exotic touch with this classic Southeast Asian combination of flavors.

1 lb 10 oz/750 g raw jumbo
  shrimp

MARINADE
1¾ cups canned coconut milk
6 tbsp chopped fresh cilantro
2 tbsp peanut oil
4 scallions, finely chopped
juice and finely grated rind of
  1 lime

TO GARNISH
lime wedges
fresh cilantro sprigs

SERVES 4

Shell and devein the shrimp, then place in a large, shallow dish. Mix together the coconut milk, cilantro, oil, scallions, and lime juice and rind in a bowl, then pour over the shrimp. Turn to coat, cover, and let marinate for 30 minutes.

Drain the shrimp, reserving the marinade. Thread them onto skewers. Grill on a medium barbecue, brushing frequently with the marinade, for 2–3 minutes on each side, or until they have turned pink and are cooked through.

Remove the shrimp from the skewers and transfer to serving plates. Garnish with lime wedges and cilantro sprigs and serve at once.

CILANTRO

These peppery shrimp make a lively and colorful dish for a barbecue.

shrimp and mixed bell pepper KABOBS

MARINADE

2 scallions, chopped

2 garlic cloves, finely chopped

1 green chili and 1 small red
   chili, seeded and finely
   chopped

1 tbsp grated fresh gingerroot

1 tbsp chopped fresh chives

4 tbsp lime juice

1 tbsp finely grated lime zest

2 tbsp chili oil

salt and pepper

KABOBS

24 large shrimp, shelled and
   deveined, but with tails left on

1 red bell pepper and 1 green
   bell pepper, seeded and cut
   into small chunks

wedges of lime, to garnish

freshly cooked rice or napa
   cabbage, to serve

SERVES 2

Put the scallions, garlic, chilies, ginger, chives, lime juice, lime zest, and chili oil into a food processor and season well with salt and pepper. Process until smooth, then transfer to a nonmetallic (glass or ceramic) bowl, which will not react with acid.

Thread the shrimp onto skewers, alternating them with the red and green bell pepper chunks. When the skewers are full (leave a small space at either end), transfer them to the bowl, and turn them in the mixture until they are well coated.

Cover with plastic wrap and let marinate in the refrigerator for 3–4 hours.

Barbecue the kabobs over hot coals for 4–5 minutes, or until the shrimp are cooked right through (but do not overcook), turning them frequently, and basting with the remaining marinade. Arrange the skewers on a bed of rice or napa cabbage, garnish with lime wedges, and serve.

sweet-and-sour POLYNESIAN

The hint of the South Pacific in this recipe gives it a charm all of its own.

SAUCE

10½ oz/300 g canned pineapple
  chunks
¼ cup soy sauce
2 tbsp sweet sherry
3 tbsp red wine vinegar
¼ cup brown sugar

KABOBS

6 slices smoked lean bacon
8 oz/225 g large shrimp, shelled
  and deveined, tails removed
1 red bell pepper and 1 orange
  bell pepper, seeded and cut
  into small chunks

freshly boiled rice, to serve

SERVES 4

To make the sauce, drain the pineapple chunks and reserve the juice.
Set the pineapple chunks aside for the kabobs. In a separate large bowl, mix
together the soy sauce, sherry, red wine vinegar, and sugar, then stir in the
reserved pineapple juice.

For the kabobs, cut the bacon slices into small pieces and wrap a piece
around each shrimp. Thread the shrimp onto skewers, alternating them with
pieces of red and orange bell pepper and the reserved pineapple chunks.
When the skewers are full (leave a small space at either end), transfer them
to the large bowl, and turn them in the mixture until they are well coated.

Barbecue the kabobs over hot coals for 8–10 minutes, or until the shrimp are
cooked right through (but do not overcook), turning them frequently, and
brushing with more sauce as necessary. Arrange the kabobs on a bed of
freshly cooked rice and serve at once.

SHRIMP

The aroma of this somewhat extravagant dish will instantly transport you to a Mediterranean beach.

lemon-marinated shrimp WITH MINT PESTO

1 lb 10 oz/750 g raw jumbo
    shrimp
juice of 2 lemons
1 bunch fresh mint, chopped
2 garlic cloves, very finely
    chopped

MINT PESTO

1 garlic clove, coarsely chopped
8 tbsp fresh mint, coarsely
    chopped
3 tbsp extra virgin olive oil
1 tbsp red wine vinegar
1 tbsp sour cream or heavy
    cream
1 tbsp grated Parmesan cheese
salt and pepper

SERVES 4

Shell and devein the shrimp. Place them in a shallow dish and sprinkle with the lemon juice, mint, and garlic. Toss well to coat, cover, and let marinate for 30 minutes.

To make the pesto, put all the ingredients in a blender or food processor and process until smooth. Scrape into a bowl, season with salt and pepper, then cover and let chill until required.

Drain the shrimp and thread them onto skewers. Grill on a medium barbecue for 2–3 minutes on each side, or until they have turned pink and are cooked through.

Remove the shrimp from the skewers and transfer to serving plates. Add a spoonful of mint pesto and serve.

barbecued TROUT

Rainbow trout occasionally needs something extra to perk up its flavor. Try it cooked this way.

4 rainbow trout, about 8–10 oz/
   225–280 g each, cleaned and
   heads removed
½ tsp crushed chilies
1 tbsp sweet paprika
1 tsp salt
4 small shallots, finely chopped
chili oil, for brushing
lime wedges, to garnish

SERVES 4

Rinse the trout inside and out under cold running water and thoroughly pat dry with paper towels.

Mix together the crushed chilies, paprika, and salt in a small bowl. Sprinkle half this mixture inside the cavities of the fish and divide the chopped shallots between them.

Brush the outsides of the fish with oil, then sprinkle with a little more of the spices. Grill on a medium barbecue, brushing occasionally with more oil and sprinkling with the remaining spices, for 4–5 minutes on each side, or until the fish is cooked through and the flesh flakes easily. Serve at once, garnished with lime wedges.

This marinade complements the delicate flavor of the fish.

barbecued SALMON

MARINADE

generous ⅓ cup vegetable oil

generous ⅓ cup dry white wine

1 tbsp molasses

1 tbsp brown sugar

1 tbsp soy sauce

1 garlic clove, chopped

pinch of ground allspice

salt and pepper

SALMON

4 salmon steaks, about 7 oz/
   200 g each

wedges of lemon, to garnish

crisp salad greens,
   to serve

SERVES 4

Put the oil, wine, molasses, sugar, soy sauce, garlic, and allspice into a large bowl and mix until well combined. Season with salt and pepper.

Rinse the salmon steaks under cold running water, then pat dry with paper towels. Add them to the wine mixture and turn them until they are well coated. Cover with plastic wrap and place in the refrigerator to marinate for at least 2 hours or overnight.

When the steaks are thoroughly marinated, lift them out, and barbecue them over hot coals for about 10 minutes on each side, or until cooked right through, turning them frequently and basting with the remaining marinade. About halfway through the cooking time, add the lemon wedges and barbecue for 4–5 minutes, turning once. Arrange the steaks on a bed of fresh salad greens, garnish with the lemon wedges, and serve.

salmon and artichoke

Wrapping fish in a package before cooking it on the barbecue keeps it marvelously succulent.

4 salmon steaks, about 6 oz/
    175 g each
½ lemon, sliced
1 onion, sliced into rings
4 fresh dill sprigs
4 canned artichoke hearts,
    drained
4 tbsp olive oil
4 tbsp chopped fresh flatleaf
    parsley
salt and pepper

SERVES 4

Cut out 4 squares of foil, each large enough to enclose a fish steak. Place the salmon on the foil and top with the lemon slices, onion rings, and dill sprigs. Place an artichoke heart on each salmon steak.

Fold up the sides of the foil. Sprinkle 1 tablespoon olive oil and 1 tablespoon parsley into each package and season with a little salt and pepper. Fold over the edges of the foil securely.

Cook the packages on a medium barbecue for 15 minutes, turning once. Transfer to serving plates, open the tops of the packages and serve at once.

PACKAGES

There's no need to marinate the fish before cooking, as the dressing provides all the flavor you need.

anchovy-topped
COD STEAKS

4 canned anchovies, drained
  and chopped
2 tbsp chopped fresh parsley
1 garlic clove, finely chopped
2 tbsp finely grated lemon rind
1 tbsp lemon juice
2 tbsp olive oil
salt and pepper
4 cod steaks, about 6 oz/
  175 g each
corn oil, for brushing

small salad, to serve

SERVES 4

Mix together the anchovies, parsley, garlic, lemon rind, and juice in a bowl, then whisk in the olive oil. Season to taste with salt, if necessary, and pepper.

Season the fish with salt and pepper and brush with corn oil. Grill on a medium barbecue, preferably in a wire barbecue basket, for 3–5 minutes on each side.

Transfer the cod steaks to 4 serving plates, spoon the anchovy dressing over them, and serve at once. Serve with a small salad.

north african SARDINES

Fresh sardines are perfect for the barbecue and taste best when they are cooked simply.

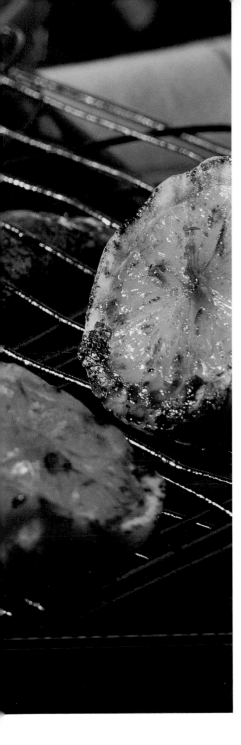

1 lb 2 oz/500 g fresh sardines,
   cleaned and scaled

grilled lemon wedges, to garnish

MARINADE
6 tbsp olive oil

3 tbsp lemon juice

3 tbsp chopped fresh cilantro

2 tsp finely grated lemon rind

½ tsp ground cumin

¼ tsp paprika

salt and pepper

SERVES 4

Place the sardines in a large, shallow dish. Mix together the olive oil, lemon juice, cilantro, lemon rind, cumin, and paprika in a bowl and season with salt and pepper. Pour the mixture over the fish, turning to coat. Cover and let stand in a cool place to marinate for 1 hour.

Drain the fish, reserving the marinade. Place the sardines in a wire barbecue basket.

Grill on a medium barbecue, brushing frequently with the marinade, for about 3 minutes on each side, or until browned. Serve at once, garnished with grilled lemon wedges.

Angler fish has a meaty texture, a delicious flavor, and no small bones to worry about.

marinated angler fish

4 angler fish fillets, about 6 oz/
175 g each

MARINADE

2 tbsp olive oil

2 tbsp chopped fresh cilantro

juice and finely grated rind of
1 lime

salt and pepper

few sprigs of fresh cilantro,
to garnish

TOMATO RELISH

1 lb/450 g plum tomatoes,
peeled, seeded, and chopped

4 dill pickles, thinly sliced

½ small cucumber, diced

2 celery stalks, thinly sliced

2 tbsp olive oil

1 tbsp white wine vinegar

1 tsp Dijon mustard

¼ tsp superfine sugar

dash of Tabasco sauce

SERVES 4

Place the fish in a large dish. Mix together the olive oil, cilantro, and lime juice and rind and season with salt and pepper. Pour over the fish, turning to coat. Cover and let marinate in a cool place for 1 hour.

Meanwhile, make the relish. Mix together the tomatoes, dill pickles, cucumber, and celery in a bowl. Whisk the olive oil, vinegar, mustard, sugar, and Tabasco in another bowl, then pour over the tomato mixture. Stir well, cover, and let stand in a cool place for at least 30 minutes.

Cut out 4 squares of foil, each large enough to enclose a fish fillet. Drain the fish, reserving the marinade, and place a fillet on each square. Fold up the sides, spoon a little marinade over each piece of fish, then fold over the foil to secure. Cook the fish packages on a medium barbecue for about 25 minutes, or until the flesh is tender and flakes easily. Open out the tops of the packages and serve at once with the relish, with the cilantro sprigs to garnish.

porgy
WRAPPED IN GRAPE LEAVES

Grape leaves protect the delicate flesh of porgy during cooking as well as imparting a subtle flavor.

2 porgy, about 12 oz/350 g each, cleaned and scaled

MARINADE
6 tbsp olive oil
2 tbsp white wine or dry sherry
2 garlic cloves, finely chopped
2 bay leaves, crumbled

1 tbsp fresh thyme leaves
1 tbsp snipped fresh chives
salt and pepper
12–16 large grape leaves

TO GARNISH
thyme leaves
half a grilled lemon

SERVES 4

Rinse the fish and pat dry with paper towels. Score both fish 2–3 times diagonally on each side and place in a large dish. Mix together the olive oil, white wine, garlic, bay leaves, thyme, and chives in a small bowl and season with salt and pepper. Spoon the mixture over the fish, turning to coat. Cover and let marinate for 1 hour.

If using grape leaves preserved in brine, soak them in hot water for 20 minutes, then rinse well and pat dry. If using fresh grape leaves, blanch in boiling water for 3 minutes, then refresh under cold water, drain, and pat dry.

Drain the fish, reserving the marinade. Wrap each fish in grape leaves to enclose. Brush with the marinade. Grill on a medium barbecue for 6 minutes on each side, brushing with more marinade occasionally.

This recipe adds a hot, spicy flavor to this highly regarded type of fish.

spicy PORGY

AÏOLI

4 large garlic cloves, finely
   chopped

2 small egg yolks

1 cup extra virgin olive oil

2 tbsp lemon juice

1 tbsp Dijon mustard

1 tbsp chopped fresh tarragon

salt and pepper

PORGY

2 porgy, filleted

2 garlic cloves, chopped

2 shallots, grated

1 small red chili, seeded and
   chopped

1 tbsp lemon juice

wedges of lemon, to garnish

TO SERVE

crisp salad greens

raw and lightly blanched
   vegetables

SERVES 4

To make the aïoli, put the garlic and egg yolks into a food processor and process until well blended. With the motor running, slowly pour in the olive oil through the feeder tube until a thick mayonnaise forms. Add the lemon juice, mustard, tarragon, and seasoning, and blend until smooth. Transfer to a nonmetallic (glass or ceramic) bowl, which will not react with acid, cover with plastic wrap, and let chill until ready to serve.

Rinse the fish under cold running water, then pat dry with paper towels. In a separate bowl, mix together the garlic, shallots, chili, and lemon juice. Rub the shallot mixture onto both sides of the fillets, then barbecue them over hot coals for about 15 minutes, or until cooked right through, turning them once. Arrange the fillets on a bed of crisp salad greens, garnish with lemon wedges, and serve separately with the aïoli and the vegetables for dipping.

red snapper WITH
ARUGULA CREAM SAUCE

The sweetness of red snapper flesh is beautifully complemented by the peppery flavor of arugula.

4 red snapper, cleaned

4 fresh rosemary sprigs

4 fresh thyme sprigs

4 fresh parsley sprigs

4 fresh fennel sprigs

olive oil, for brushing

lemon slices, to garnish

ARUGULA CREAM SAUCE

4 oz/115 g arugula

2 tbsp butter

4 scallions, finely chopped

2 tbsp all-purpose flour

⅔ cup milk

⅔ cup heavy cream

1 tsp lemon juice

salt and pepper

SERVES 4

Rinse the fish inside and pat dry with paper towels. Place a sprig of each herb inside the cavities. Brush the fish with olive oil, place in a wire barbecue basket, and set aside.

To make the sauce, blanch the arugula in boiling water for 5 minutes. Drain, refresh under cold water, then drain again. Pat dry with paper towels and finely chop. Set aside.

Melt the butter in a pan over low heat and cook the scallions, stirring occasionally, for 3–5 minutes, or until softened. Stir in the flour and cook, stirring constantly, for 1 minute. Remove from the heat and gradually stir in the milk, followed by the cream. Return to the heat and bring to a boil, stirring constantly. Let simmer for 2–3 minutes, or until thickened.

Remove from the heat, stir in the arugula and lemon juice and season with salt and pepper. Place on the side of the barbecue to keep warm.

Grill the fish on a medium barbecue for 3–4 minutes on each side, brushing with more olive oil if necessary. Serve at once, garnished with lemon slices, with the sauce spooned over.

This colorful dish is packed with Mediterranean flavors and looks every bit as good as it tastes.

red snapper WITH

2 shallots, finely chopped

2 garlic cloves, finely chopped

4 tbsp chopped fresh parsley

½ cup pine nuts,
   coarsely ground

3 tbsp olive oil

6 red snapper, cleaned

1 yellow bell pepper, seeded and
   cut into strips

6 tomatoes, peeled, seeded, and
   cut into strips

2 tbsp butter, diced

salt and pepper

SERVES 6

Mix together the shallots, garlic, chopped parsley, and pine nuts in a bowl
and gradually beat in the olive oil.

Cut out 6 squares of foil, each large enough to enclose a fish. Rinse the fish
and pat dry on paper towels. Place a fish on each square of foil and spread
the pine nut and herb mixture evenly over them. Divide the bell pepper strips
between them and top with the tomato strips. Dot with the butter.

Fold up the sides of the foil to enclose the fish and fold over the edges to
secure. Cook the packages on a medium barbecue for about 25 minutes, or
until the fish is tender and the flesh flakes easily. Open the tops of the
packages and serve.

BELL PEPPERS AND TOMATOES

lightly seared tuna WITH

The fashionable way to serve tuna is just seared on the outside and very rare in the center, like steak.

1 lb 2 oz/500 g tuna steak, about
   3 inches/7.5 cm thick
finely grated rind and juice of
   1 lemon
salt and pepper

small salad, to serve

SAUCE VIERGE

½ cup extra virgin olive oil
juice of 1 lemon
4 ripe tomatoes, peeled, seeded,
   and chopped
2 garlic cloves, finely chopped
2 tbsp chopped fresh parsley
2 tbsp chopped fresh chives
1 tbsp chopped fresh tarragon

SERVES 4

Place the tuna steak in a large dish and sprinkle over the lemon rind and juice. Season with salt and pepper, cover, and let chill until required.

To make the sauce, mix together the oil, lemon juice, tomatoes, and garlic in a bowl. Season with salt, cover, and let stand for 2 hours.

Stir the chopped herbs into the sauce. Remove the tuna from the marinade and cook on a hot barbecue for 2–5 minutes on each side, depending on how rare you like it.

Transfer the tuna to a serving platter and spoon over half the sauce. Cut the fish into thick strips and serve at once, offering the remaining sauce separately. Serve with a small salad.

SAUCE VIERGE

This marinade really complements the flavor of the tuna fish.

tuna and tarragon
SKEWERS

MARINADE
2 tbsp white wine

3 tbsp balsamic vinegar

1 tbsp extra virgin olive oil

1 garlic clove, finely chopped

salt and pepper

SKEWERS
10½ oz/300 g fresh tuna steaks

1 lb/450 g white mushrooms

chopped fresh tarragon,
  to garnish

TO SERVE
freshly cooked rice

mixed salad

SERVES 4

Put the wine, vinegar, olive oil, and garlic into a large bowl and mix until well combined. Season with salt and pepper to taste.

Rinse the tuna steaks under cold running water and pat dry with paper towels. Cut them into small cubes. Wipe the mushrooms clean with paper towels. Thread the tuna cubes onto skewers, alternating them with the white mushrooms. When the skewers are full (leave a small space at either end), transfer them to the bowl, and turn them in the wine mixture until they are well coated. Cover with plastic wrap and place in the refrigerator to marinate for at least 30 minutes.

Barbecue the skewers over hot coals for about 10 minutes, or until the tuna is cooked right through (but do not overcook), turning them frequently, and basting with the remaining marinade. Arrange the skewers on a bed of rice, garnish with chopped fresh tarragon, and serve with a mixed salad.

vegetarian **AND** salads

Vegetarians often feel left out at barbecues, feeling them to be very meat-oriented. Nothing could be further from the truth. Vegetarian food is versatile and diverse, and works extremely well when cooked on the barbecue. Enjoy experimenting with new ingredients and combinations, especially the more unusual and exotic fruit and vegetables that are now so widely available. This section provides some delicious vegetarian dishes that will tempt even the most hardened of carnivores, and some interesting salads, which make excellent accompaniments.

This mild cow's milk cheese and vegetable recipe goes well with the simple marinade.

provolone cheese
AND VEGETABLE KABOBS

MARINADE
4 tbsp extra virgin olive oil

2 tbsp balsamic vinegar

2 garlic cloves, finely chopped

1 tbsp chopped fresh cilantro

salt and pepper

KABOBS
8 oz/225 g provolone cheese

12 white mushrooms

8 pearl onions

12 cherry tomatoes

2 zucchini, cut into small chunks

1 red bell pepper, seeded and
  cut into small chunks

chopped fresh cilantro,
  to garnish

TO SERVE
freshly cooked rice or salad
  greens

fresh crusty bread

SERVES 4

Put the oil, vinegar, garlic, and cilantro into a large bowl. Season with salt and pepper and mix until well combined.

Cut the provolone cheese into bite-size cubes. Thread the cubes onto skewers, alternating them with whole white mushrooms, pearl onions, cherry tomatoes, and zucchini and red bell pepper chunks. When the skewers are full (leave a small space at either end), transfer them to the bowl, and turn them in the mixture until they are well coated. Cover with plastic wrap and place in the refrigerator to marinate for at least 2 hours.

When the skewers are thoroughly marinated, barbecue them over hot coals for 5–10 minutes, or until they are cooked to your taste, turning them frequently, and basting with the remaining marinade. Arrange the skewers on a bed of freshly cooked rice or fresh mixed salad greens, garnish with cilantro leaves, and serve with fresh crusty bread.

spicy vegetable KABOBS

A zesty barbecue sauce adds plenty of flavor as it's brushed over the vegetables during cooking.

4 tbsp Worcestershire sauce

4 tbsp peanut oil

4 tbsp tomato ketchup

1 tbsp red wine vinegar

1 tbsp brown sugar

1 tsp English mustard

6 cherry tomatoes

3 red bell peppers, seeded and
   quartered

6 open cap mushrooms,
   quartered

2 small red onions, cut into
   wedges

3 zucchini, cut into 1½-inch/
   4-cm chunks

salt and pepper

SERVES 6

Mix the Worcestershire sauce, oil, ketchup, vinegar, sugar, and mustard
together in a bowl, stirring well to combine.

Thread the vegetables alternately onto 6 skewers and brush them all over
with the sauce.

Grill the vegetable kabobs on a medium barbecue, turning and brushing
frequently with the sauce, for 10–12 minutes, or until the vegetables are
tender. Serve at once.

Mushrooms and pears make a unique combination for these tasty skewers.

vegetarian mushroom

MARINADE
2 tbsp extra virgin olive oil
1 tbsp balsamic vinegar
1 garlic clove, finely chopped
salt and pepper

SKEWERS
1 lb 10 oz/750 g mycroprotein
   pieces or fillets, cut into
   small chunks

SERVES 4

1 lb/450 g white mushrooms
1 large pear, cored and cut into
   small chunks

wedges of pear, to garnish

TO SERVE
fresh green and red lettuce
   leaves
fresh crusty bread

Put the oil, vinegar, and garlic into a large bowl. Season with salt and pepper and mix until well combined.

Thread the mycroprotein (Quorn) pieces onto skewers, alternating them with the mushrooms and pear chunks. When the skewers are full (leave a small space at either end), transfer them to the bowl, and turn them in the mixture until they are well coated. Cover with plastic wrap and place in the refrigerator to marinate for at least 1 hour.

Barbecue the skewers over hot coals for about 5 minutes, or until the mycroprotein is cooked right through, turning them frequently and basting with the remaining marinade. Arrange the skewers on a bed of fresh green and red lettuce leaves, garnish with wedges of pear, and serve with fresh crusty bread.

AND PEAR SKEWERS

bean and vegetable
BURGERS WITH TOMATO SALSA

These burgers will become a firm favorite with children.

BURGERS

7 oz/200 g canned chickpeas,
    drained and rinsed
7 oz/200 g canned cannellini
    beans, drained and rinsed
1 large zucchini, finely grated
1 large carrot, finely grated
1 garlic clove, finely chopped
⅔ cup fresh bread crumbs
salt and pepper

SALSA

4 large tomatoes, chopped
1 tbsp lime juice
2 shallots, chopped
1 garlic clove, chopped
1 tbsp chopped fresh basil

TO GARNISH

chopped fresh basil
wedges of lime

hamburger buns, to serve

SERVES 4

Put the chickpeas and cannellini beans into a food processor and blend
together briefly. Transfer to a large bowl, then add the zucchini, carrot, garlic,
and bread crumbs. Season with salt and pepper, then mix together until
thoroughly combined. Using your hands, form the mixture into burger
shapes, transfer to a shallow dish, and cover with plastic wrap. Let chill for
30 minutes.

To make the salsa, put the tomatoes, lime juice, shallots, garlic, and basil
into a bowl and stir together. Cover with plastic wrap and set aside.

Barbecue the burgers over hot coals for 5–10 minutes on each side, or until
cooked right through. Remove from the coals and transfer to serving plates.
Garnish with chopped basil and wedges of lime and serve with hamburger
buns and the salsa.

An exciting variation on the burger theme gives a tasty dish that will be popular with all.

chili bean burgers WITH

SALSA

4 large tomatoes, chopped

1 red onion, finely chopped

1 garlic clove, chopped

1 tbsp chopped fresh cilantro

1 tbsp chopped fresh flatleaf
  parsley

1 tbsp red wine vinegar

1 tbsp lime juice

salt and pepper

BURGERS

8 oz/225 g red kidney beans

1 large carrot, boiled and
  mashed

1 large red onion, finely chopped

½ cup fresh bread crumbs

4 tbsp all-purpose flour

1 tbsp tomato paste

sprigs of fresh cilantro and
  wedges of lime, to garnish

hamburger buns and vegetarian
  cheese slices, to serve

SERVES 4

To make the salsa, put the tomatoes, onion, garlic, herbs, vinegar, and lime juice into a bowl. Season with salt and pepper and mix until well combined. Cover with plastic wrap and set aside.

To make the burgers, drain the canned kidney beans, rinse them, and drain them again. Put them into a large mixing bowl with the carrot, onion, bread crumbs, flour, and tomato paste, and mix until well combined. Season well with salt and pepper. Using your hands, form the mixture into burger shapes. Barbecue the burgers over hot coals for 5–10 minutes on each side, or until cooked right through. Garnish with sprigs of fresh cilantro and wedges of lime and serve with hamburger buns and cheese slices.

ONION SALSA

mixed nut burgers
WITH CHILI

Three types of nut combine to make these tasty burgers.

scant 1 cup boiling water

2 tbsp soy sauce

1¾ cups bulgur wheat

generous ⅝ cup cashews

generous ⅝ cup hazelnuts

generous ¼ cup almonds

1 garlic clove, grated

1 small red chili, seeded and
   finely chopped

1 tsp dried mixed herbs

1 tbsp tomato paste

4 eggs

TO SERVE

hamburger buns

slices of tomato

chopped mixed nuts, toasted

SERVES 4

Pour the boiling water and soy sauce into a heatproof bowl. Rinse and drain the bulgur wheat three times, then add it to the bowl and stir into the liquid. Let stand for 15–20 minutes, or until all the liquid has been absorbed.

While the bulgur wheat is soaking, grind the cashews, hazelnuts, and almonds in a food processor. When the bulgur wheat is ready (and all the liquid has been absorbed), add the ground nuts to the bowl, and stir them in. Then add the garlic, chili, mixed herbs, tomato paste, and eggs and mix until well combined. Cover with plastic wrap and let chill for 3 hours.

When the mixture has chilled, form it into burger shapes, then barbecue over hot coals for 10–12 minutes, or until cooked through, turning once. About halfway through the cooking time, add the tomato slices. Barbecue for 4–5 minutes, turning once. Serve at once with hamburger buns, the tomato slices, and chopped nuts.

These tasty vegetarian sausages are very simple to make.

spicy VEGETARIAN SAUSAGES

SERVES 4

Put the garlic, onion, chili, mashed kidney beans, bread crumbs, almonds, rice, and cheese into a large bowl. Stir in the egg yolk and oregano, then season with salt and plenty of pepper.

Using your hands, form the mixture into sausage shapes. Roll each sausage in a little flour, then transfer to a bowl, cover with plastic wrap, and let chill for 45 minutes.

Brush a piece of aluminum foil with oil, then put the sausages on the foil and brush them with a little more vegetable oil. Transfer the sausages and foil to the barbecue. Barbecue over hot coals, turning the sausages frequently, for about 15 minutes, or until cooked right through. Serve with hotdog rolls, cooked sliced onion, and tomato, and tomato ketchup and/or mustard.

1 garlic clove, finely chopped

1 onion, finely chopped

1 red chili, seeded and finely chopped

14 oz/400 g canned red kidney beans, rinsed, drained, and mashed

1¾ cups fresh bread crumbs

generous ¼ cup almonds, toasted and ground

¾ cup cooked rice

1¾ oz/50 g Cheddar cheese, grated

1 egg yolk

1 tbsp chopped fresh oregano

salt and pepper

flour, for dusting

vegetable oil, for brushing

TO SERVE

fresh hotdog rolls

sliced onion, lightly cooked

sliced tomato, lightly cooked

tomato ketchup and/or mustard

vegetable SATAY

Colorful vegetable kabobs are delightful served with a slightly crunchy peanut sauce.

MARINADE

3 zucchini, cut into 1-inch
  2.5-cm chunks
1 eggplant, cut into 1-inch/
  2.5-cm chunks
8 baby corn
8 white mushrooms
3 tbsp peanut oil
3 tbsp lime juice

SATAY SAUCE

¾ cup canned coconut milk
scant ½ cup crunchy
  peanut butter
2 tsp dark soy sauce
1 tsp brown sugar
pinch chili powder

SERVES 4

Put the zucchini and eggplant chunks, corn cobs, and mushrooms in a bowl.
Mix together the oil and lime juice in a pitcher and pour over the vegetables.
Stir well, cover, and let marinate for 4 hours.

To make the satay sauce, pour the coconut milk into a small pan and stir in
the peanut butter. Heat gently, stirring constantly, until smooth. Stir in the
soy sauce, sugar, and the pinch of chili powder. Transfer to the side of the
barbecue to keep warm.

Drain the vegetables, reserving the marinade, and thread them alternately
onto 4 skewers. Grill on a medium barbecue, turning occasionally for about
10 minutes. Serve at once, with the satay sauce.

Here's a taste of Mexico with these inventive tortillas.

stuffed TORTILLAS

SERVES 2

Cook the red bell peppers on the barbecue, skin-side down, for about 5 minutes, or until the skins are blackened and charred. Transfer them to a plastic bag, seal the bag, and set to one side.

Barbecue the sausages over hot coals for 10–12 minutes, or until cooked right through, turning occasionally. While the sausages are cooking, put the kidney beans, tomatoes, onion, garlic, lime juice, and basil into a large bowl. Season with salt and pepper and mix until well combined.

Take the red bell pepper quarters from the plastic bag and remove the blackened skins. Chop the flesh into small pieces and add it to the kidney bean mixture. About 1 minute before the sausages are ready, warm the tortillas on the barbecue for a few seconds.

Remove the sausages from the barbecue and cut them into slices. Fill the tortillas with sausage slices, kidney bean salsa, shredded lettuce, tomato slices, and sour cream. Serve at once with a salad garnish.

4 vegetarian sausages

SALSA
2 red bell peppers, seeded and
   cut into quarters
11½ oz/325 g canned red kidney
   beans, drained, rinsed, and
   drained again
4 large tomatoes, chopped
1 large onion, chopped
1 garlic clove, chopped
1 tbsp lime juice
1 tbsp chopped fresh basil
salt and pepper

4 large wheat or corn tortillas,
   or 8 small ones

salad, to garnish

TO SERVE
shredded lettuce
slices of fresh tomato
sour cream

vegetable packages

These packages make a great vegetarian main course or a hot accompaniment to a meat dish.

2 red onions, sliced into rings

2 zucchini, sliced

1 eggplant, sliced

1 red bell pepper, seeded
   and sliced

1 orange bell pepper, seeded
   and sliced

1 green bell pepper, seeded
   and sliced

8 oz/225 g cremini mushrooms

4 tsp chopped fresh thyme

4 tbsp olive oil

salt and pepper

SHERRY VINEGAR DRESSING

1 tbsp sherry vinegar

3 tbsp extra virgin olive oil

1 garlic clove, finely chopped

salt and pepper

SERVES 4

To make the dressing, put the sherry vinegar, olive oil, and chopped garlic in a screw-top jar, season with salt and pepper, close the lid, and shake vigorously. Set aside in a cool place until required.

Cut out 4 large squares of foil. Divide the vegetables between them, heaping them up in the center. Sprinkle with the thyme and season with salt and pepper. Fold up the sides of the foil, sprinkle 1 tablespoon olive oil in each package, then fold over the edges to seal.

Cook on a medium barbecue for 8–10 minutes, turning the packages occasionally. Open out the packages and transfer the contents to serving plates. Sprinkle with the dressing and serve.

WITH SHERRY VINEGAR DRESSING

These filled baps make great food for an informal party outdoors.

cheese AND VEGETABLE BAPS

2 red bell peppers, seeded and
  cut into quarters
2 zucchini, sliced
1 large onion, cut into rings
5½ oz/150 g baby corn
3 tbsp olive oil
4 large white or whole-wheat
  baps, halved horizontally to
  make 8 thinner circles
4 oz/115 g cured firm cheese,
  grated

sour cream, to serve

SERVES 4

Cook the bell peppers on the barbecue, skin-side down, for 5 minutes or until the skins are charred. Transfer them to a plastic bag, seal the bag, and set to one side. Brush the zucchini, onion rings, and corn with oil and barbecue over hot coals for 5 minutes, turning them frequently and basting with more oil if necessary.

While the vegetables are on the barbecue, take the bottom halves of the baps, brush the cut sides with oil and sprinkle over some cheese. Cover with the top halves, then wrap each bap in foil and transfer them to the barbecue. Warm for 2–4 minutes, just until the cheese starts to melt (do not overcook).

While the baps are warming, take the bell pepper quarters from the bag and remove the skins. Chop the flesh into small pieces and transfer it to a plate with the other vegetables.

Transfer the baps to serving plates and remove the foil. Fill them with the cooked vegetables and sour cream and serve at once.

carrot, cabbage,
AND MIXED FRUIT SALAD

Here is a cool, tasty accompanying dish for a hot barbecue.

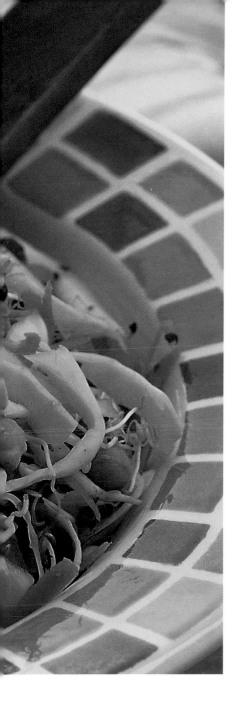

7 oz/200 g raw carrots
7 oz/200 g raw white cabbage
3½ oz/100 g beansprouts
1¾ oz/50 g alfalfa sprouts
generous ¼ cup golden raisins
generous ¼ cup raisins
1 tbsp lemon juice

SERVES 4

Trim and peel the carrots, then grate them into a large salad bowl. Trim the white cabbage, then shred it finely. Transfer it to a large strainer and rinse under cold running water. Drain well, then add it to the carrots.

Put the beansprouts and alfalfa into the strainer and rinse well, drain, and add to the salad. Rinse and drain the golden raisins and raisins and add to the bowl. Pour in the lemon juice and toss the salad in it, then serve.

A favorite salad for an outdoor meal.

beet, apple, and CELERY SALAD

2 apples
2 large or 4 small cooked beets
2 celery stalks
generous ⅓ cup plain yogurt
1 tbsp lemon juice

SERVES 4

Wash and core the apples, but leave the skin on. Grate them into a large salad bowl.

Grate the beet, then add it to the bowl with the apples. Wash and trim the celery stalks, cut them into small pieces, then add them to the salad.

Add the yogurt and lemon juice, mix until all the ingredients are thoroughly combined, then serve.

potato, arugula, AND
MOZZARELLA SALAD

A delicious combination of ingredients makes this a fresh and appealing salad.

1 lb 7 oz/650 g small new
   potatoes
4½ oz/125 g arugula leaves
5½ oz/150 g firm mozzarella
1 large pear
1 tbsp lemon juice
salt and pepper

DRESSING
3 tbsp extra virgin olive oil
1½ tbsp white wine vinegar
1 tsp sugar
pinch of mustard powder

SERVES 4

Bring a pan of salted water to a boil. Add the potatoes, reduce the heat and cook for about 15 minutes, or until tender. Remove from the heat, drain, and set aside to cool.

When the potatoes are cool, halve them, and place them in a large salad bowl. Wash and drain the arugula leaves, cut the mozzarella into cubes, and wash, trim, and slice the pear. Add them to the bowl along with the lemon juice. Season with salt and pepper.

To make the dressing, mix together the oil, vinegar, sugar, and mustard powder. Pour the dressing over the salad and toss all the ingredients together until they are well coated. Serve at once.

The variety of textures of the different ingredients makes this a very enjoyable salad.

avocado, corn, AND

12 oz/350 g canned corn

½ cup walnuts, chopped

2 large, ripe avocados

6 tbsp lemon juice

6 tbsp sour cream

2 tbsp walnuts, chopped,
   to garnish

SERVES 4

Drain the corn, then put it into a large salad bowl. Add the walnuts and mix
until well combined.

Peel, pit, and cut the avocados into small pieces, brush them with some of
the lemon juice to prevent discoloration, then add them to the salad.

In a separate bowl, mix the remaining lemon juice with the sour cream until a
smooth consistency is reached. Add more lemon juice or cream if necessary.
Add the lemon cream to the salad, stir it in, sprinkle with chopped walnuts,
and serve.

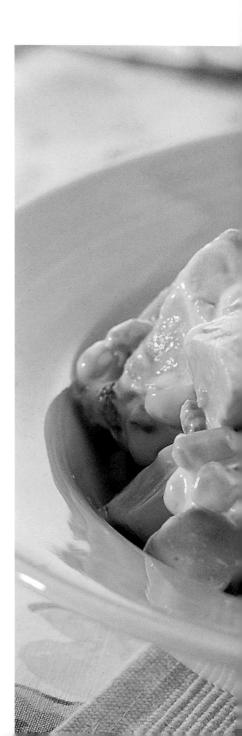

WALNUT SALAD

tabbouleh

This popular Lebanese dish was traditionally served with lamb, but goes well with all barbecued food.

1¾ cups bulgur wheat

½ cucumber

4 ripe tomatoes

3 scallions

3½ oz/100 g fresh flatleaf
   parsley

3½ oz/100 g fresh mint

juice of ½ lemon

chopped fresh parsley,
   to garnish

TO SERVE

4 pita breads

wedges of lemon

SERVES 4

Rinse and drain the bulgur wheat three times, then transfer it to a large
heatproof bowl.

Bring a kettle of water to a boil. Pour over enough boiling water to cover
the bulgur wheat, with about ½ inch/1 cm more on top. Set aside for
15–20 minutes, or until the water has been absorbed.

While the bulgur wheat is soaking, prepare the salad. Peel the cucumber, cut
it into small cubes, and transfer it to a large salad bowl. Wash and chop the
tomatoes and trim and chop the scallions, then add them to the bowl. Wash
and chop the herbs, and add them to the salad with the lemon juice.

When the bulgur wheat is ready, squeeze out any remaining moisture, and
add it to the salad. Toss all the ingredients together and garnish with
chopped parsley. Warm the pita breads on the barbecue for a few seconds,
then pass them round with the tabbouleh. Serve with wedges of lemon.

fava beans WITH
MOZZARELLA AND BASIL

This is a very simple salad to make.

1 lb/450 g fava beans
  (shelled weight)
4 tbsp extra virgin olive oil
1 tbsp lime juice
1 tbsp finely chopped fresh basil
2¼ oz/60 g firm mozzarella

TO GARNISH
finely chopped fresh mint
wedges of lime

SERVES 4

Bring a pan of water to a boil, then add the fava beans and cook for
2 minutes. Drain well and let cool. In a separate bowl, mix together the olive
oil, lime juice, and chopped basil.

When the beans are cool, transfer them to a large salad bowl. Pour over
the dressing and mix until well combined. Cut the mozzarella into cubes
and stir them gently into the salad. Garnish with chopped fresh mint and
lime wedges.

Here is a spicy variation on a tomato salad.

spicy tomato SALAD

4 large ripe tomatoes
1 small red chili
1 garlic clove
1 oz/25 g fresh basil
4 tbsp extra virgin olive oil
1 tbsp lemon juice
2 tbsp balsamic vinegar
salt and pepper

TO GARNISH
sprigs of fresh basil
wedges of lemon

fresh crusty bread, to serve

SERVES 4

Bring a kettle of water to a boil. Put the tomatoes into a heatproof bowl, then pour over enough boiling water to cover them. Let them soak for 2–4 minutes, then lift them out of the water and let cool slightly.

When the tomatoes are cool enough to handle, gently pierce the skins with the point of a knife. You should now find them easy to remove. Discard the skins, then chop the tomatoes and place them in a large salad bowl.

Seed and finely chop the chili, then chop the garlic. Wash and finely chop the basil, then add it to the tomatoes with the chile and the garlic.

In a separate bowl, mix together the oil, lemon juice, and balsamic vinegar, then season with salt and pepper. Pour the mixture over the salad and toss together well. Garnish with basil sprigs and lemon wedges, and serve with fresh crusty bread.

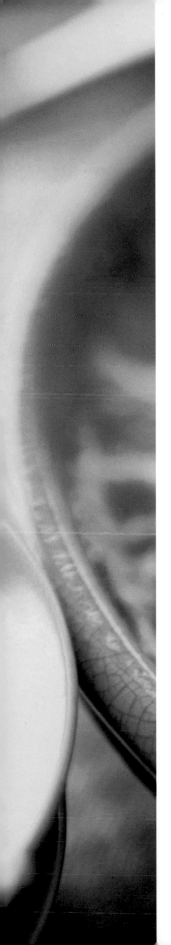

desserts

People often don't associate desserts with barbecuing, but think again. It makes sense, having barbecued the entire meal, to prepare a quick, easy, and healthy dessert using the same method of cooking. This section contains some fruit recipes that are simple yet elegant, such as apple and melon kabobs; others are more indulgent, such as barbecued bananas smothered in chocolate with a dash of rum added. Most importantly, all are simple to prepare and cook.

A delicious way to cook summer fruits.

summer fruit NECTARINES

4 large nectarines

7 oz/200 g frozen summer fruits
(such as blueberries and
raspberries), thawed

3 tbsp lemon juice

3 tbsp honey

sour cream, mascarpone
cheese, or ice cream, to serve

SERVES 4

Cut out eight 7-inch/18-cm squares of aluminum foil. Wash the nectarines,
cut them in half, and remove the pits. Place each half-nectarine on a square
of foil.

Fill each half-nectarine with summer fruits, then top each one with
1 teaspoon of lemon juice, then 1 teaspoon of honey.

Close the foil around each half-nectarine to make a package, then barbecue
them over hot coals for about 10–15 minutes, according to your taste. Remove
from the barbecue, place the half-nectarines on serving plates, and serve at
once with sour cream, mascarpone cheese, or ice cream.

barbecued APPLES

Apples bake to perfection on the barbecue, making a delightful dessert for any meal.

4 apples, such as Granny Smiths'

3 tbsp lemon juice

3 tbsp butter

4 tsp brown sugar

8 tbsp sweet mincemeat (raisins,
    apples, and spices)

plain yogurt, sour cream, or
    mascarpone cheese, to serve

SERVES 4

Wash the apples, then cut them in half from top to bottom. Remove the cores
and pips, then brush the cut sides of the apples with lemon juice to prevent
discoloration.

Put the butter in a small pan and gently melt it over low heat. Remove from
the heat, then brush the cut sides of the apples with half of the butter. Set
aside the rest of the melted butter.

Sprinkle the apples with sugar, then transfer them to the barbecue, cut-sides
down, and cook over hot coals for about 5 minutes. Brush the apples with the
remaining butter, then turn them over. Add 1 tablespoon of mincemeat to the
center of each apple, then cook for an additional 5 minutes, or until they are
cooked to your taste.

Remove from the heat and transfer to serving plates. Serve at once with
plain yogurt, sour cream, or mascarpone cheese.

This is a perfect way to end a barbecue as it requires almost no effort at all to prepare.

grilled apples WITH
GIN AND GRAPEFRUIT SAUCE

4 eating apples

2 oz/55 g unsalted butter

4 tbsp gin

3 tbsp superfine sugar

6 tbsp grapefruit juice

SERVES 4

Thread each apple onto a skewer and grill on a medium barbecue, turning frequently, for 15–20 minutes, or until cooked through.

Meanwhile, melt the butter in a pan on the barbecue. Add the gin, sugar, and grapefruit juice and stir until the sugar has dissolved. Keep the sauce warm on the side of the barbecue.

Transfer the apples to serving plates and serve the sauce on the side for dipping.

Why not end your barbecue with a deliciously tropical finale of hot kabobs glazed with a creamy sauce?

fruit kabobs
WITH SPICY RUM CREAM

1 tbsp rum

2 tbsp superfine sugar

¼ tsp ground cinnamon

1 cup mascarpone cheese

2 lb 4 oz/1 kg tropical fruits, such
    as mango, papaya, bananas,
    kiwifruit, and pineapple, cut
    into even chunks

juice of 1 lime

2 tbsp brown sugar

SERVES 4

Mix together the rum, superfine sugar, and cinnamon in a bowl, stirring until
the sugar has dissolved. Stir in the mascarpone.

Thread the fruit chunks alternately onto skewers. Brush the fruit well with
lime juice.

Grill on a medium barbecue for 2–3 minutes on each side. Sprinkle with the
brown sugar and grill for an additional 1 minute. Serve at once, with the
spicy rum cream.

Bananas are very sweet when barbecued, and conveniently come in their own protective wrapping.

chocolate rum BANANAS

1 tbsp butter

8 oz/225 g semisweet or milk
  chocolate

4 large bananas

2 tbsp rum

grated nutmeg, to decorate

sour cream, mascarpone
  cheese, or ice cream, to serve

SERVES 4

Take four 10-inch/25-cm squares of aluminum foil and brush them
with butter.

Cut the chocolate into very small pieces. Make a careful slit lengthwise in
the peel of each banana, and open just wide enough to insert the chocolate.
Place the chocolate pieces inside the bananas, along their lengths, then
close them up.

Wrap each stuffed banana in a square of foil, then barbecue them over hot
coals for about 5–10 minutes, or until the chocolate has melted inside the
bananas. Remove from the barbecue, place the bananas on individual
serving plates, and pour some rum into each banana.

Serve at once with sour cream, mascarpone cheese, or ice cream, topped
with nutmeg.

Grilling fruit brings out its full flavor and makes it simply irresistible on a summer's evening.

caramelized FRUIT MEDLEY

1 fresh pineapple

1 ogen melon

⅔ cup sweet sherry

generous ½ cup superfine sugar

1½ cups large strawberries

SERVES 4

Cut the pineapple into thick slices across. Cut off the peel with a small sharp knife, then, holding each slice upright, cut out the "eyes." Stamp out the core from each slice with an apple corer. Halve the melon and scoop out the seeds with a teaspoon. Cut into thick wedges and peel with a sharp knife.

Mix the sherry and sugar together in a large dish, stirring until the sugar has dissolved. Add all the fruit and toss well to coat. Cover and let marinate in a cool place for 2 hours.

Drain the fruit, reserving the marinade. Grill the pineapple on a hot barbecue for 4 minutes, then turn over and brush with the marinade. Add the melon and grill for 2 minutes, then turn over and brush with the marinade. Add the strawberries and grill for 2 minutes. By this time, the fruit should all be golden and juicy. Serve at once.

brandied pineapple RINGS

The smooth sweetness of the brandy complements the sharpness of pineapple.

1 pineapple, peeled, cored, and
   cut into rings

MARINADE
2 tbsp honey
3 tbsp brandy
2 tsp lemon juice
fresh mint sprigs, to decorate

SERVES 4

For the marinade, put the honey, brandy, and lemon juice into a large, nonmetallic (glass or ceramic) bowl, which will not react with acid. Stir together until well combined.

Put the pineapple rings into the bowl and turn them in the mixture until thoroughly coated. Cover with plastic wrap, transfer to the refrigerator, and let marinate for 1–1½ hours.

When the pineapple rings are thoroughly marinated, lift them out, and barbecue them over hot coals for about 10 minutes, turning them frequently and basting with more marinade if necessary.

Remove the pineapple rings from the barbecue, arrange them on individual serving plates, and decorate with fresh mint sprigs.

Stuffed figs are a real treat for any barbecued meal.

stuffed FIGS

8 fresh figs

scant ½ cup cream cheese

1 tsp ground cinnamon

3 tbsp brown sugar

fresh mint sprigs, to decorate

plain yogurt, sour cream,
    mascarpone cheese, or ice
    cream, to serve

SERVES 4

Cut out eight 7-inch/18-cm squares of aluminum foil. Make a small slit in each fig, then place each fig on a square of foil.

Put the cream cheese in a bowl. Add the cinnamon and stir until well combined. Stuff the inside of each fig with the cinnamon cream cheese, then sprinkle a teaspoon of sugar over each one. Close the foil round each fig to make a package.

Place the packages on the barbecue and cook over hot coals, turning them frequently, for about 10 minutes, or until the figs are cooked to your taste. Transfer the figs to serving plates and decorate with fresh mint sprigs.

Serve at once with plain yogurt, sour cream, mascarpone cheese, or ice cream.

Index